Praise for *The Almighty Dollar*

'Original and engaging . . . If you've ever wondered
what globalisation is and why people get so passionate
about it then I can think of no better guide. Economics
can be fascinating and accessible. This book is proof.'
Joel Hills, Business Editor, ITV News

'Brilliantly revealing.'
**Ian King, business presenter, Sky News,
and *Times* columnist**

'A brilliant book . . . everyone should buy
it because it's very, very readable.'
Iain Dale, LBC

'Readable and illuminating.'
The Bookseller

Environomics

How the Green Economy is Transforming Your World

Dharshini David

Elliott&Thompson

First published 2024 by
Elliott and Thompson Limited
2 John Street
London WC1N 2ES
www.eandtbooks.com

ISBN (hardback): 978-1-78396-629-5
ISBN (trade paperback): 978-1-78396-676-9

9 8 7 6 5 4 3 2 1

A catalogue record for this book is available from
the British Library.

Typesetting: Marie Doherty

Printed by CPI Group (UK) Ltd, Croydon, CR0 4YY

Contents

Introduction   vii

1   Switching on the Lights   1
    The energy revolution taking place in our homes

2   Getting Dressed   27
    Overcoming our addiction to fast fashion

3   Checking Your Phone   53
    Protecting the rare resources consumed by technology

4   Receiving a Parcel   69
    *Untangling the complex web of the global shipping
    network*

5   The Daily Commute   89
    Swapping petrol for electricity

6   Buying a Coffee   115
    Overhauling plastics and the disposable lifestyle

7   At Work   135
    *Investments, finance and how businesses are going
    green*

8   Time for Lunch   155
    Balancing one of life's necessities – food – with its
    environmental impact

9   Making a Purchase   183
    The hidden cost of how we pay

10 Heading Home   195
    Living in a world of concrete and steel

11 Sushi for Dinner   215
    Protecting the oceans from overfishing and more

12 The Weekly Shop   229
    Ending our reliance on palm oil

Acknowledgements   247
A Note on Sources   249
Index   251

Introduction

Economics and climate change are more closely linked than you might realise – and they have a greater impact on your life too. When you order your morning coffee, for example, do you like sugar with that? Well, it will cost you.

In 2024, sugar prices rose to their highest for well over a decade, driven by droughts in some of the world's biggest exporting countries. These droughts were one of the consequences of the extreme heat seen in 2023, the hottest year on record, where global temperatures are estimated to have been more than 1.5 per cent above pre-industrial averages. Other effects of this heat were more sobering: over 11,000 lives lost in a flood in Libya; a record area of forests devastated by fires in Europe and Canada. Such events are occurring with increasing frequency.

Industrialisation and globalisation have brought us choice, lower prices and more affordable lifestyles, and have pulled millions out of poverty. But these forces have expanded so rapidly, particularly over the second half of the twentieth century, that they have had undesirable consequences too, not least driving our seemingly unquenchable thirst for fossil fuels. The sprawling concrete megacities and belching coal power stations in China, the massive mining operations in the Democratic Republic of the Congo or Brazil, the ships built to traverse the Pacific in days to serve our growing appetites – all of these come at an environmental cost. So too do the SUVs, gadgets and meat-heavy diets we've come to rely on. All of these typical features of our modern twenty-first-century lives have contributed towards those increasingly worrying climate 'events'.

With every disaster, we hear fresh cries for more to be done to curb climate change, along with howls of despair that sufficient efforts aren't being made. In late 2023, even as world leaders met in Dubai for COP 28 (Conference of the Parties, the annual United Nations Climate Change Conference) researchers were warning that global emissions from fossil fuels had reached an unprecedented high (and that's before considering the planes needed to jet to in nearly 100,000 delegates to that conference).

There was much talk there, and everywhere else, of what action we need to take to reduce our carbon emissions, tackle the amount of waste and pollution we create, clean up the plastics in our seas and save the biodiversity of our planet, while, at the same time, agonising over when – or whether – we'll get there.

Many countries and organisations have adopted the target of becoming carbon neutral, reducing the amount of carbon dioxide their processes add to the atmosphere to virtually zero, or somehow balancing – in effect cancelling – that amount through carbon offsetting or carbon capture (more on those later). The Paris Agreement, adopted in 2015 by 193 countries plus the EU bloc, goes further. It vowed to pursue efforts to limit global temperature rises to below 1.5°C, to restrict *all* greenhouse gas emissions – not just carbon emissions – to the same amount that can be absorbed naturally (commonly known as net zero), to set country-based emission-reduction targets and to help out poorer countries. But the agreement didn't address *how* to do this. That is where economics comes in.

It's impossible to understand how this journey can progress without an economic perspective, because nearly every issue that affects the environment comes down, in some way, to what someone, somewhere, is doing to make (or save) money, to make a living. Changes to the way people do business are propelled by economic need and so are completely intertwined with the way we live our lives. There are costs to manage if benefits are to be delivered – and unintended consequences to consider if we are to nurture economies and livelihoods.

And so green issues are revolutionising our economy. In every major industry we are seeing changes driven by efforts to be greener. This is a truly global story involving vast, complex supply chains, technological innovations, commercial interests, foreign policy, corporate investment. But it doesn't just affect businesses and governments, it impacts all of us in the simplest, most fundamental aspects of our lives. How we power our homes, how we move about, the food we eat – all of it is changing. Economics isn't just a load of dull men (or even women) in suits talking about statistics on the radio – it's the very fabric of our lives, the physical world that we touch, taste, smell every day.

I wanted to bring that global green revolution to life in a way that makes sense to us all, that we can all relate to. So I've explored, chapter by chapter, our typical daily routines, from groping for the light switch and getting dressed to the daily commute and the buildings we inhabit, and how these everyday habits and actions are affected by the economic changes taking place. And, in turn, how our actions can also affect what is happening in those industries.

As I noted in my first book, *The Almighty Dollar*, it's easy for us as individuals to feel powerless and at the mercy of overwhelming economic forces, driven by global powers, governments and major corporates. The same may feel true of environmental action too – and sometimes it is true; certain decisions are out of our control. But we can all play a part in influencing outcomes. Even simple things such as the toothpaste or shampoo we choose to buy can make a difference, while other decisions we make can influence companies and governments, nudging them to do the right thing.

And so, as we'll see, change is being driven by numerous players. It's changing consumer habits that made Vinted, the web-based marketplace set up by a woman in Lithuania to clear out her wardrobe, into a billion-dollar resale platform with over a hundred million users in fifteen years. Investor pressure and concerns about obsolescence amid a fast-changing environment have nudged the oil and gas majors into investing in renewables, and manufacturers and retailers to focus on circularity. States have played a role too, stepping in where the market won't or to chivvy things along – with his 2022 Inflation Reduction Act, President Biden boasted of the 'largest investment in clean energy and climate action ever'.

Real progress is being made. At COP 28, negotiators from all nations agreed for the first time on the need to 'transition away from fossil fuels in energy systems' – a major breakthrough. Some were frustrated by the lack of an explicit target for phasing them out, and loopholes in the final text. Bad news sells: journalists are fully aware that our audiences tend to have a 'negativity bias' and are more likely to focus on what's going awry rather than what's working out, which is possibly why there was more emphasis on that aspect than the positive steps, but they were made nonetheless. Also in 2023, the Inflation Reduction Act swung into full force, prompting similar action from other governments. A treaty to protect the oceans, forty years in the making, was agreed. The rate of deforestation in the Amazon slowed, after the Brazilian government vowed to phase out the practice by 2030.

There is of course much further to go. Many say the targets on the table are not enough. If we carry on as we are, some estimates suggest that we would need the equivalent resources of three Earths by 2050 to maintain today's living standards. It's easy to feel disheartened when reading about climate change and the dangers to our planet, especially given some of the recent global challenges. The last decade has not been one of business as usual, but rather 'polycrisis': the Covid-19 pandemic followed by wars that have destabilised global energy and food supply markets, and so wreaked havoc with financial well-being. It can be difficult to fathom how action on climate change finds a place in all this. But change often begets change, and some of the various crises have also prompted positive developments.

Covid-19 may have created billions of pieces of plastic waste from all the face masks and other protective gear needed but it also normalised remote working, meaning fewer commuter journeys, and prompted companies to move their supply chains closer to the place of production. The energy crisis may have caused some to double down on fossil fuel extraction in the short term, to keep the lights on, but it also encouraged energy conservation, and a greater focus on renewables to secure future energy supply. A cost-of-living crisis may have pushed some environmental measures down the priority list for both households and politicians – the UK government, for example, has pushed back the phasing out of sales of new petrol cars – but it also inspired a thriftier, make-do-and-mend mindset.

This book doesn't pretend to have definitive answers to our challenges, but it strives to be a guide to how things are working, what's motivating the various players and why it should matter to you. Governments are acting. Technology is advancing. Our long-formed habits are changing. Looking at what exactly is happening can inject a little optimism, as well as identifying the areas that still need work and where the challenges are. It also reveals what we can do as individuals and where we need to rely on policy, the profit motive and corporate conscience. Getting there may not be easy – and it will depend on everyone knowing the part they must play – but we are heading in the right direction.

As I started researching this book, I realised, simply looking around the room, that my perspective on the world was shifting. Every single thing that we use, that we encounter in our daily lives, requires some kind of energy, produces some kind of waste, and involves a long, complex list of materials and processes to make. The new green imperatives are aiming to change much of that, and so even the simplest items and routines in our lives can tell a bigger story: a fast-moving global story of change – and resistance to change. This book is a guide to understanding those shifting tides.

1

Switching on the Lights

The energy revolution taking
place in our homes

As the alarm goes off, you roll over and blearily switch on the light. And so begins your energy usage for the day. Early bird or late riser, for most of us the meter starts running the moment our eyes flicker open in the morning. There's the heating clicking on, the hot water for the shower, the kettle for that much-needed cup of coffee. All those little morning rituals that get your day going depend on energy. And that energy was probably produced in a huge power station, belching out fumes, because, in most developed countries, the majority of our homes are currently powered by fossil fuels. But maybe not for much longer.

Fossil fuels – coal, oil, gas – account for about 80 per cent of the world's energy use, from electricity generation and home heating to transportation and the manufacture of steel and plastic. They are carbon-rich non-renewable resources: essentially a stored form of solar energy, created through pressure and temperature over many millions of years. Carbon is one of the key drivers of climate change and one of the main pollutants clogging up our atmosphere.

How much of it is down to the energy use of the average person in the street? A government survey in the UK in 2022 found that one in three people thought that the actions of large polluters should be tackled before individuals, and a similar proportion reckoned that changing their own behaviour would make little difference.

And yet, the same study found that households are responsible for over a quarter of greenhouse gas emissions. Energy usage is calculated in kilowatt hours (kWh): one kilowatt hour is equivalent to powering a 100W light bulb for ten hours. The average household in Britain is estimated to use around 15,000 kWh of energy a year on powering their home, most of which is accounted for by heating and hot water. This isn't to let major corporations and governments off the hook, but that figure suggests that as individuals we can still make a difference. It's tricky, though, to see exactly where we can make changes; our modern lifestyle is energy hungry, so while as individuals we can be mindful of turning off lights and unplugging appliances, ultimately we do still need to heat our homes, see where we're going, wash our clothes. We don't have all that much say in where our power comes from. That's down to energy companies and government policy. And, for now, both are heavily reliant on the use of fossil fuels.

The story of fossil fuels actually isn't as straightforward as it looks. Although at first sight they might seem to be the supervillains in the climate change drama, for many years they have enabled us to live richer, longer and better lives. We've become addicted to them because they have been the drivers of our prosperity – superheroes without which the modern world could not exist. Over the last 200 years, global GDP has tracked energy use, and the more energy we've used, the wealthier and healthier we've become. Even after the crisis in global energy prices in 2022, weaning ourselves off them can feel like an impossible dream; none of us is prepared to switch off the lights, give up our televisions and go back to washing all our clothes by hand.

Yet energy transitions have happened before. Our relationship with fossil fuels has been relatively brief, given the span of human history. As our needs have increased over time, we've seen several shifts in fuels and energy sources, usually driven by scarcity, price and availability. And we're in the midst of another change right now.

Prior to the Industrial Revolution, which began in the mid-eighteenth century, lumber, animals, wind and water provided most of the energy people needed for heat and transport. As populations grew, lumber became scarce, wind and water insufficient, and living closely with so many animals created a huge amount of waste and they became a source of pollution and disease.

These problems were solved by coal. Coal mining really took off in the Elizabethan Age in the UK but it took a few hundred years more for coal to become the linchpin of industrial progress and transportation. It came into its own with the rise of the steam engine, which could run on wood or coal. However, being three times as energy intensive as wood, weight for weight, and cheaper to boot, coal had the upper hand. By 1900, it was the main industrial fuel. The Industrial Revolution lifted millions out of poverty and set them on the road to rising living standards. Coal had a valuable role in the transformation of our lives. But it is also the filthiest member of the fossil fuel family. Coal mining causes toxic run-off into waterways. The sulphur and nitrogen emitted when it is burned causes acid rain.* Coal power stations also account for a fifth of global greenhouse gas emissions. That makes coal twenty times as toxic across its life cycle as solar energy and about seventy times as toxic as wind power.

But even before concerns about its environmental impact went mainstream, another even more transformative source of power was emerging. Despite being millions of years in the making, crude oil has been part of our lives on a mass scale for less than 200 years. The first commercial well resulted from Edwin Drake's Pennsylvania explorations in 1859. A plentiful supply allowed for rapid industrialisation and the rise of the USA as a global economic powerhouse. By the early 1900s, the second major energy transition was under way, driven literally by the popularity of the passenger car (see Chapters 4 and 5). By the 1960s oil had superseded coal as the world's leading energy source, being twice as energy intensive as its rival. The expansion of the oil industry also led to an increased supply of natural

---

* Any form of precipitation with lowered pH levels, which can damage natural environments, human-made structures and human health.

4

gas, which is often found and extracted alongside oil, and has become a mainstay of many a nation's energy source.

Concurrently, a domestic revolution was starting from the smallest but most illuminating of household objects – the electric light bulb. From the 1870s onwards, that drove households into the light, and sealed the popularity of electricity, which was typically generated from . . . fossil fuels.

So our rising living standards and all the comforts and convenience that the twentieth century brought to developed countries were entirely thanks to the plentiful supply of coal, oil and gas. Our dependence on these superheroes was such that governments around the world have subsidised extraction and development as a way of boosting their economies. Affordable coal, oil and gas enabled economic development and a more prosperous way of life.

But even as life got better for many, there was a heavy price to pay. By the start of the twentieth century, the side effects of rapid industrialisation were hard to ignore: acrid clouds of smoke hovered menacingly over cities, and bronchitis was a major source of fatalities in the UK. Across the USA, women who were yet to get the vote formed various smoke-abatement associations, in protest at the blighted air.

Muttered about in scientific circles for as long as a century before, the darker side of fossil fuels went prime time in 1988, when climate scientist James Hansen warned US Congress that global warming was primarily due to greenhouse gases built up in the atmosphere due to the burning of those sources of energy.

You'd think that might have spurred widespread change – but public awareness grew very slowly. In the early twentieth century, the discovery, exploration and distribution of oil and gas in the Middle East gave rise to the Seven Sisters: mega companies that controlled the market and the industry. They were the forebears of America's Exxon and Chevron, Europe's BP and Royal Dutch Shell. Today, the power has shifted to largely state-owned enterprises that represent the biggest oil producers: Saudi Aramco, Gazprom of Russia, Brazil's Petrobras, for example. As the evidence on climate change has mounted, many of the biggest energy firms have adopted a business-as-usual strategy: keep on churning for as long as the wheels keep on turning.

And their efforts have gone further than that, initially denying their role in climate change and later lobbying heavily for continued government support on the basis that they are crucial to sustaining Western economies, world economic growth and jobs. In 2018, the big five – Shell, BP, Exxon, Chevron and ConocoPhillips – stood accused by activists of spending close to $200 million trying to influence or block climate change legislation, or just change the narrative. Some of those companies, including Exxon, contested the claim, saying that there were different ways of dealing with the risks of climate change, and that there was also a danger of equating policy debate and disagreement with climate disinformation. Behind the scenes, energy bosses have been known to argue that without the replacement infrastructure – the electric vehicles, the replacement of boilers with heat pumps – realistically customers will be reliant on fossil fuels for some time. And they, of course, are perfectly placed to serve that need. Moreover, some of their shareholders are likely to be unforgiving if companies miss a chance to beef up profits. As our economies thunder on and our global population grows, appetite for energy is not diminishing, and some of the companies that supply it may be inclined to resist change.

But while fossil fuels are still the primary source of our energy, thanks to the usual factors of price and availability – and thirst for profit – that's no longer the only driving force for change. Increasingly there's a growing desire to do better by the planet and its people. Which means that those natural market forces might need a helping hand.

〜

While each country has a different 'energy mix' – Japan, for example, has been heavily reliant on fossil fuels, while France's main power source is nuclear – the push towards renewables has been visible across the globe. Taking the UK as an example, in 1960, 90 per cent of the nation's power was generated by coal. By 1990 it had fallen to 67 per cent. Renewables didn't really get a look in until this point but then things started to change drastically. By 2022 coal accounted for just 1.5 per cent of the UK's energy mix, while renewables had risen to 40 per cent.

That change was driven by price competition and the growing availability of alternatives, but also by the government helping the transition to less filthy alternatives. Of course, we didn't jump straight from coal to renewables. What first allowed the country to move away from its coal dependence was gas, and that's a common transition story around the world.

As far back as the mid-twentieth century, coal was being targeted in the UK by Clean Air Acts of 1956 and 1968 after smog became as much of a feature of London as the iconic double-decker red bus. After the Second World War, a new variety of pipelines had made the delivery of natural gas to cities more viable – and therefore an accessible source for domestic heating.

While the UK is a gas producer, about half of its gas comes from abroad, in part due to a lack of storage and refining capacity. The key source of imports is from Norway, via pipeline, with some of the rest coming in a liquid form, for example from Qatar. One of the downsides of gas, though, is that supply is vulnerable and the price can skyrocket, as happened following the invasion of Ukraine, with Russia threatening to withhold its gas supplies. Russia is one of the world's biggest producers, second only to the USA. Only 3 per cent of the UK's gas came from there in 2021, but as the country has to compete for gas supplies from abroad, it's subject to variations in global gas prices. With the likes of the EU trying to wean itself off Russian gas (which made up a third of its imports in 2021), those prices spiked in 2022.

The other downside to gas is that it is still a fossil fuel and, while cleaner than coal, it does still produce harmful emissions. So, even while the UK was transitioning to gas, the hunt was on for an alternative.

Cue nuclear energy. Uranium atoms are split to create heat; the resulting steam is used to power generators and so produce electricity. The world's first major electricity-generating nuclear power station opened in the UK in 1956. By 1996, nuclear powered around a quarter of the country's electricity, and more than one-sixth globally.

Unlike fossil fuels, it produced no greenhouse gases. Efficient, cheap, clean – or so it was thought. But its flaws soon became apparent. Nuclear power is not a renewable energy source; it relies on uranium, of which there's likely to be enough for another couple of centuries, but it will eventually run out. What's more, nuclear plants have a finite working life of perhaps forty years, but some don't make it that far. The USA has retired five plants early because they were no longer econom-ically viable. It isn't simply the case of replacing clapped-out, overpaid assets with cheaper, younger models. Over-budget and over time has increasingly become the signature of the twenty-first-century nuclear plant. That's particularly true of the new generation of safer and more efficient plants. In fairness, that is true of most public-investment projects; getting the green light seems habitually to mean presenting an enticingly low estimate that rarely ends up being realistic.

There was also the issue of nuclear waste and how to dispose of it safely. In the event of an accident the resulting radioactive material could cause widespread and lasting havoc. Chernobyl and Fukushima have become shorthand for the devastation, mutation, illness and death caused by nuclear disasters. In the case of the latter, an earthquake and tsunami prompted nuclear meltdown and thousands of deaths. As a result, there was a pause in the use of many nuclear reactors in Japan and a rethink in many nations around the globe.

But it was relatively short-lived. In 2022, the spike in fos-sil fuel prices caused by Russia's invasion of Ukraine and the resulting focus on energy security proved to be a game changer. The British government announced the great nuclear revival, with a target to triple the amount of energy generation by nuclear by 2050. Legislation in the USA prompted up to $40 billion of estimated subsidies for the industry, to prop up existing reactors and support new ones. That sort of incentive might be needed, given how expensive they are; the first US reactor built from scratch in three decades, in Georgia, cost far more than initially budgeted and took far longer to build than expected.

In 2022, the International Energy Agency increased its projection for global nuclear power, expecting capacity to double by 2050, meaning that it would account for around 14 per cent of electricity generation. With the problem of how to dispose of nuclear waste still unresolved, nuclear remains a far more risky and pricey way of powering the planet than renewables. It costs five times as much to generate nuclear power than wind or solar. But with a lack of large-scale alternatives as yet, nuclear remains an option for now for governments hoping to bridge the energy transition.

The most dramatic change to our energy sources, however, has been a result of a revolution that started quietly in the 1970s. The oil-price crisis that created waves of unrest around the world also fuelled interest and investment in wind and solar technology.

In 1974, Saudi Arabia, the leading light in OPEC – the organisation of oil-producing nations – attempted to influence the price of oil by turning the production taps on and off. At that time OPEC was so powerful that the threat of an embargo towards any country suspected of supporting Israel in the Yom Kippur War saw the price of a barrel quadruple from $3 to $12. That caused a seismic shock throughout the oil-consuming world. By then oil was an intrinsic part of the manufacturing and transportation process. The cost of living spiralled, unions demanded higher wages in response and economies were driven backwards into recession.

It did, however, push nations to rethink their power supplies and reduce their dependence on oil imports. Denmark, for example, switched power plants from oil to coal. That might not sound like progress in terms of cleaner energy but, after

10

all, energy security is as important as food security. That was not the only change taking place. Response from business was dynamic too: energy efficiency, which had already been making gains since the end of the Second World War, took on a new lease of life. Investment in technology that improved energy efficiency or made use of alternative fuels, which had previously been considered too expensive, suddenly became relatively affordable in comparison to the high oil price. The result was that production processes became more resilient and economies were better insulated when it came to swings in the price of energy, such as the spike that followed Russia's invasion of Ukraine in 2022.

The oil-price shock of the 1970s shook the world and left a lasting legacy. Back then, wind and solar power on a mass scale was a pipe dream, but the more money that went into the technology, the more realistic it became. The first wind farm in the USA was installed in 1980; the UK followed just over a decade later. Unlike in previous transitions, however, the new sources produced less energy and couldn't fulfil the demand, meaning the market needed a helping hand. From Brussels to Beijing, the state has played an increasing role in driving the transition, filling the gaps the market has (sometimes) been reluctant to. In China's case, that meant direct state spending. In more market-driven economies, governments have often subsidised the development of greener energies, while at the same time – and as a way of funding that injection – penalising the generation of fossil fuels, for example through schemes such as Europe's Emissions Trading System (whereby power generators face a cap on emissions and have to pay for carbon 'permits' – see page 169).

Despite government help, the growth of the wind and solar industries has faced obstacles along the way. In the UK, national planning policy means that since 2015 fewer than one in eight local authorities have allocated space for onshore wind farms. And the ones that do get built may prove controversial. Take Viking, one of the UK's largest wind farms, with over a hundred turbines, each 155 metres tall. It was built by energy giant SSE on the Shetland Islands, one of the windiest parts of the country. The area has benefited hugely from the North Sea oil industry, but when the oil starts running dry, becoming a hub for wind power could help offset some of those potential losses. However, construction meant digging deep concrete foundations into previously untouched peatland and building access roads that disrupted the landscape, much to the resentment of some residents. Reaping the rewards of decarbonisation comes with its own costs.

Even the plants that are built and raring to go can have problems offloading their energy. The UK's transmission mechanism network is privately owned by the National Grid. But that network has a limited capacity, and applications to join have more than quadrupled since 2018. Under the first-come-first-served planning rules slated by many as archaic, some applicants who are ready and able to supply renewable energy now aren't able to hook up because they're still waiting for a permit, stuck in the queue behind a project that has stalled. Some have been told they will have to wait a decade or more before they can connect. The National Grid blames the planning system as well as regulations that have prevented it from scaling up capacity fast enough. In 2023 the operators promised an overhaul, whereby projects with little chance of success would be pushed further back in the queue.

The cost of constructing a wind farm is another major hurdle. For those costs are front-loaded, even if the running costs are relatively marginal. How to entice operators, then, to invest and build given that prices paid for energy can vary?

In the UK, when the government allocates licences for offshore wind farms, it sets an electricity price. Energy suppliers can bid for the licence to supply electricity at that price, which is then guaranteed for fifteen years. In September 2023, the auction was set with a guarantee of £44 per megawatt hour but it failed to attract a single bid, with even offshore giants such as SSE and Sweden's Vattenfall declaring early on that it wasn't an attractive bet. Industry representatives said that spiralling steel prices, a key component in wind farms, and higher wages meant that costs had risen by around a third since an earlier successful auction with a similar target was held.

And there are other ways in which changing tack isn't plain sailing. For example, supply of the technology for wind and solar can be problematic. In China's drive to become the world's leading industrial nation, it's become the global leader in the production of solar panels, wind turbines and grid technology. Nine out of ten solar cells hail from China and it's a major producer of polycrystalline silicon – or polysilicon – which is an integral part of most solar cells. The problem? Over 40 per cent of the world's current supply of comes from the Xinjiang regime of China, where, following studies from the UK's University of Sheffield Hallam and others, the USA's Bureau of International Labor Affairs declared that forced labour is rife. Manufacturing polysilicon itself is fairly energy intensive; a cheap and plentiful supply of coal-powered electricity was what established Xinjiang as a major source of supply. Green, it seems, isn't always clean.

Despite these obstacles, rapid development at scale and technological advances meant that a tipping point for renewable energy was reached in the twenty-first century.

Globally, renewable energy costs have fallen rapidly, which means that renewables have become a more attractive alternative to fossil fuels. In the USA in 2019, wind and solar generation costs dipped to new lows, falling by 70 per cent and almost 90 per cent respectively over a decade, undercutting the cost of coal (using a measure that considers the total cost of building and operating capacity over its lifetime). That trend seems set to continue. In 2022, over a fifth of the USA's electricity was generated from renewable sources, overtaking coal as a source for the first time. A quarter of its wind power comes from Texas alone; a future reboot of the soap *Dallas* may feature turbines in the place of those oil barons and their Stetsons.

It is not just in the USA. In 2018 wind powered 17.1 per cent of UK electricity; by 2022 it was nearly 27 per cent. In that year, renewables made up a record 40 per cent of electricity generation – but fossil fuels still had the edge. There still isn't enough of a renewable supply to meet demand.

However, there's nothing like an energy security scare to focus minds. Governments scrabbling to compensate for Russian supplies haven't just pushed for more fossil fuel energy. At the end of 2022 the International Energy Agency concluded:

The global energy crisis is driving a sharp acceleration in installations of renewable power, with total capacity growth worldwide set to almost double in the next five years, overtaking coal as the largest source of electricity generation along the way and helping keep alive the possibility of limiting global warming.

That's as much renewable capacity as had been added in the previous twenty years – or as much as needed to power China.

Wind and solar form a central part of policies such as President Biden's $369 billion Inflation Reduction Act, which contains the most significant climate legislation in US history. By investing in domestic energy production and manufacturing, incorporating tax breaks for electric vehicles, heat pumps, batteries, nuclear power, clean hydrogen generation, and wind and solar energy, the policy aims to reduce carbon emissions by roughly 40 per cent by 2030. But it brought cries of foul play from Europe and beyond, as nations were afraid their industries would be disadvantaged as US players enjoyed state subsidies. Concerns arose that, in the race to build green infrastructure, sky-high commodities prices would result, causing more bumps in the journey to develop wind and solar power further.

Ultimately, however, wind and solar power do have limitations – for example, when it comes to energy density.* Refined oil is one billion times more energy dense than wind power and the figure is even higher when it is compared to solar. That means vastly more space is required to harness those sources of energy than for fossil fuels. While wind and solar generation on a massive scale is firmly under way, using them to replace fossil fuels in their entirety is not yet viable.

But if fossil fuels are on their way out, there needs to be a mass-scale alternative we can turn to. What are our options?

---

* The amount of energy that is released by a certain quantity of the fuel source.

There's nuclear, of course, but it has its drawbacks, as we've seen. Is there a magical elixir out there that can provide plentiful, effective, cheap and environmentally friendly energy?

Hydropower, effectively harnessing the energy emitted by water as it moves, has been around since the third century BCE and remains globally a key source of renewable energy. But it too is limited in its capacity as dams are expensive to build. Moreover, damming a river comes with considerable environmental impacts – from disturbing the biodiversity of waterways to creating carbon emissions from the decomposing plant and animal material diverting waterways creates.

Biomass – fuel from an organic source such as plants – is another alternative, but it too is relatively expensive and comes with environmental side effects. Plants are space intensive; large-scale farming can cause deforestation; and ultimately the fuel is still nowhere near as efficient as fossil fuels.

One option that has become the holy grail for many is hydrogen. It is seen as having huge potential. Bankers at Goldman Sachs think it could supply a quarter of the world's energy by 2050. We'll delve into the technology in Chapter 4, where we'll see it has the potential to power industry, ships and planes, reaching the parts of our economies that electrification can't. When it comes to the way we heat and power our homes, it also has the potential to replace gas; the infrastructure could be integrated into existing gas pipelines. For now, it remains expensive and inefficient compared with more conventional fossil fuels. But with countries from Japan to Germany to South Korea publishing hydrogen strategies, and the UK's energy infrastructure body developing plans to update the country's gas network, that could change rapidly.

More investment is needed to develop this potential new superhero – and once more the market needs help to get there. Because while there's still plentiful demand for fossil fuels, companies will still invest in them.

⌇

Big energy companies might seem to be moving incredibly slowly when it comes to making the shift, reluctant to give up their focus on fossil fuels, but in 2014 it transpired that one energy giant had been factoring potential climate-change-mitigation measures into its commercial decisions for some time. In 1981, a chemical engineer employed by ExxonMobil to look into the viability of developing a massive gas field off the coast of Indonesia warned that the reserve was 'mainly CO_2, the main driver of climate change'. The engineer went on to ponder the impact possible regulatory action to curb carbon emissions could have on the bottom line.

However, it wasn't the link between its products and global warming that was behind the company's hesitation. In fact, it continued to play down that link for many years after that. For Exxon, the problem with the gas field was that it might one day become a 'stranded asset'. Put simply, the huge investments in their core business that energy companies have made over the years will become useless, devalued, as regulation and availability of alternatives make them less economically viable.

Stranded assets fast became a reality in the first couple of decades of this century. European and US energy giants wrote down close to $150 billion of them in the first nine months of 2020, according to the *Wall Street Journal*. And, to comply with the Paris Agreement goals of restricting global temperature increase, far more may have to be shelved. Analysts struggle to estimate exactly how much but the total could exceed $1 tril-lion. It's coal rather than oil that would make up the majority of those assets because, primarily, it's the dirtiest, which means it's an easy target as many governments up their climate goals. But it would also be about a third of the value of the oil majors.

Exxon is dragging its feet over replacing its money-spinners; its investment in renewables is minimal, focusing instead pri-marily on reducing emissions from its own operations. It claims there are 'tremendous opportunities' to use its 'technology and expertise' in carbon capture and storage. It is the world leader in carbon capture, a market analysts reckon is set to be worth trillions of dollars.

But many rivals, particularly European ones, are realising that survival means becoming 'integrated' companies. BP, Shell and Total, for example, have boosted investment in low-carbon alternatives on a major scale. BP has said it will increase the amount it invests in renewables tenfold to $5 billion by 2030. That would be the equivalent of 14 per cent of its total capital expenditure, although, as of 2022, it was lagging behind Shell and Total. Is it enough? Should it be making a greater commit-ment? Is it too little too late? In 2019, BP paid out $8 billion to shareholders, sixteen times as much as it invested in renew-ables that year – and still more than it intends to invest in 2030. However, BP is the only oil major that has a target to cut output of fossil fuels, set at a quarter of its 2019 levels by 2030.

Environmental groups too have queried the investment fig-ures of some of the oil majors; low carbon, after all, simply means lower emissions than fossil fuels typically produce. One

claimed, for example, that some of Shell's 'renewable' investments are actually geared towards gas. Shell claimed in response
that it met regulatory requirements.

The transition for these companies might be painful, but it's
not impossible. In 2018, Norway's largest company changed
its name from Statoil to Equinor, to reflect its rapidly changing strategy. It followed a decision to earmark 15–20 per cent
of its capital investment for renewables, placing it far ahead of
most rivals. Companies often change names to shake off a reputational problem. In Equinor's case, it was trying to pre-empt
what it saw as the inevitable negative connotations of the word
'oil' in the future. Two-thirds owned by the Norwegian government, it perhaps had less reason than most large energy
companies to tease investors with a green makeover.

But it had another motive. Behind every energy success
story, behind every transition, lies highly skilled personnel; the
energy industry is nothing without human capital. But students
have been increasingly unwilling to train for careers in the oil
and gas industry. Surveys showed Statoil was dropping down
the ranks of students' favoured places to work; the indications
were that Equinor might have a better chance of wooing them.

Of course, looks aren't everything. Equinor's primary
activities remain in the field of fossil fuels. For all the talk of
supercharging investment in renewables, particularly wind, such
sources will account for only about 10 per cent of its energy
provision by 2030. But it's a move in the right direction.

It's a direction in which Denmark has already outrun most
competitors. For decades, the company DONG (Danish Oil
and Natural Gas) was the country's dirty secret, accounting for
a third of the nation's carbon emissions. Denmark's electricity

generation was one of the most carbon intensive in Europe; in 2009, 85 per cent of its energy came from fossil fuels. By the time DONG changed its name to Ørsted in 2017, it had embarked on a huge turnaround, instigated by fear of carbon pricing and a wish to do the right thing.

The CEO of Ørsted's offshore-wind business, Martin Neubert, has recounted how it was public opposition to a new coal-fired power station, along with the realisation that the pro-ject couldn't be completed sustainably, that made the company realise that change was needed. It was a bumpy ride, battered along the way by internal resistance, political pressures and headwinds from the financial crisis. But having sold its fossil fuel assets and invested heavily, by 2020 it was the king of off-shore wind, providing 30 per cent of global supply.

Since floating on the stock market in 2014, its shares have out-performed those of many rivals as it ticked the right boxes with investors. It's become a case study in successful transition, albeit one that can't be readily replicated. Far larger companies, for example, have many more assets that cannot be easily offloaded. Others might not have windy shores at their disposal – or the right expertise. When Ørsted decided to make the switch, the company was already involved in wind projects across Europe.

And it's worth remembering that fossil fuel assets don't dis-appear when sold; they are just run by other companies. But it shows what can be done with determination, and political and investor support.

Denmark consequently became the first fossil-fuel-producing country to cease new exploration projects in the North Sea, a key plank of a commitment to phase out fossil fuel production by 2050. It's a bold move; almost fifty years in the oil business has made Denmark one of the richest countries in Europe. By the government's own admission, ceasing new exploration will cost almost £2 billion in forgone revenue.

But where's there's political will, there's a way. Denmark's government aims to produce 100 per cent of its electricity from greener sources by 2030. It's spurred on the country to become the global leader not just in wind power but in the efficient integration of renewables into its energy supply system, while maintaining a reliable power grid. It might have come with a considerable upfront price tag, but in the long run Denmark's focus on transition may pay off.

~

Government backing has encouraged investment in greener energy. Energy companies are beginning to move in the right direction, albeit very slowly. What can consumers do to help things along?

To an extent there isn't a huge amount the average person can do. We have little individual say in where our energy comes from. The measures available to install in our own homes are not always within financial or practical reach. Solar panels have become a lot cheaper but a quality system will still cost thousands of pounds to install in the UK. Bearing in mind the vagaries of the British weather, that system could take upwards of a decade to pay for itself. But as they should have a life-span of at least double that, they should pay in the long term. However, that is assuming you have a suitable roof and don't mind it being covered with panels. And that you plan on staying in the same home for that length of time.

What about your own personal wind turbine? It's an option for which US homeowners can get some government help, but the results are variable and unreliable; the turbines themselves can be noisy and, for some, unsightly. The investment is not certain to pay off.

Another solution is installing a heat pump, which runs on electricity. It is a one-metre cube attached to the side of your home that transfers heat from the ground outside to warm up the inside of a property in winter. It can do the same in reverse in the summer, acting as a cooling system (a bit like a refrigerator on a human scale). As they don't create heat, they're typically more efficient than furnaces.

However, not every home is suitable for a heat pump system. For those that are, installation can cost around £15,000. In theory, the extra outlay should be recouped, but only over many years. The UK has attempted to defray by offering considerable subsidies for those looking to install heat pump systems, but the upfront payment is still large for a technology that is unfamiliar to most homeowners and whose effectiveness might be in question, given that some of those who have taken the leap complain of inadequate heating. And although heat pumps use a third of the energy that a gas boiler does, because they run on electricity, which costs more than gas, the bills could actually be higher when the price of electricity spikes. So overall the incentive to switch to a pump is extremely low.

How about getting the energy companies to do the work? One hundred per cent green tariffs are increasingly available for British customers – but they don't mean that the energy you're getting is renewable. What arrives through the wires depends on the mix in your area on that particular day; all electricity comes from the National Grid, so there is likely to be a blend from many sources. Such a tariff may mean only that the energy supplier has purchased 'renewable certificates' to cover the value of your energy consumption. These are meant to provide money for other generators to invest in renewable production; your energy provider isn't actually required to have purchased that amount of renewable energy itself. As customers become more aware of the loophole, a small but increasing number of suppliers are offering tariffs underpinned by a guarantee that they are buying that amount of renewable energy directly from another supplier to go onto the grid, or themselves investing in renewable generation.

Things are changing but individual choices are still limited when it comes to powering your home. For those concerned, the simplest action, for now, may be to continue to limit consumption as much as possible with energy-saving habits and measures, whether that's improving the insulation of homes or turning off the lights when leaving a room, and to seek clarity from energy providers.

∽

It's clear that, this time around, price and availability are not the only drivers of the energy transition we need. To get suppliers and customers on board, policies such as the European Green Deal, a €1 trillion package that aims to make the EU climate neutral by 2050, are needed. That raises an important question: who should pay for the energy transition?

The recent success of the renewables sector – with wind and solar power now cheap enough to compete with fossil fuels

– means that some are asking whether governments should still be artificially lowering their costs. Others would argue yes, as a measure to speed the transition to green and meet nations' climate change goals.

If much of the funding and support for these transitions is coming from governments, then essentially that means it's tax-payers who will be footing the bill. And governments' ability to push for the energy transition is based on what its voters are willing to tolerate.

Carbon taxes, for example, are designed to penalise pol-luting companies, but they target only Scope 1 and Scope 2 emissions – those produced by the company's own operations. Scope 3, which includes those emissions that result from the use of its products – i.e., those generated by consumers – are not covered. How much more will consumers be willing to pay, as these emissions come under the microscope?

Arguably, many existing taxes already place the burden on consumers. For example, the UK's 'green' tax on electricity is applied to all customers, and the lower the household's income, the larger the burden relative to that income; such taxes can be seen as unfair and may be unpopular. The cost-of-living crisis that began in 2022 brought this into sharp relief, with some pol-iticians querying if customers should be laden with extra costs for benefits that would be felt largely by future generations. Arguably those benefits will be significant enough for us to feel it's worth it – but in reality it's a tough sell to families struggling to put food on the table.

Then there are costs to decommissioning the more traditional sources of energy. Shutting a coal plant – which typically has a lifespan of 40 or 50 years – might come with a bill of between

$5 and $15 million, from paying for demolition to dealing with environmental issues such as cleaning up coal storage areas, which can make up a substantial proportion of the costs. The EU reckons weaning itself off coal might cost 160,000 jobs by 2030, a quarter of which would be in Poland. Not all will or can be replaced by green jobs; governments will have a role to play in enabling the transition. Denmark's momentous decision to stop oil and gas production, for example, had to make provision for those workers who were going to lose out.

Timing is also a key issue here. The transition must be a coordinated effort between government, energy companies and consumers for it to work. If energy generators make the switch before the proper infrastructure is in place to allow consumers to wean themselves off fossil fuels, for example, the result will be a major imbalance between supply and demand, which could cause further extreme price spikes.

There are reasons to be cautious but also reasons for optimism. The advance of renewables has been rapid this century; change can happen. Electrification will be a key way of reducing our dependence on fossil fuels. To push the green revolution forward, we shall need a massive increase in the amount of clean electricity generated by other sources: wind, solar, nuclear, hydrogen and other emerging solutions further investment might produce.

There's a new generation of superheroes waiting in the wings, and governments and investors are all working to get them into the limelight. But, as any fan of superhero franchises knows, eliminating the wrongdoers takes time, patience and considerable effort, with many a twist along the way.

While you won't see it when you switch that light on, there's a fast-moving energy revolution happening right now.

2

Getting Dressed

Overcoming our addiction to fast fashion

There's no putting it off any longer, it's time to get dressed. But why does it feel so impossible to find something to wear, when your wardrobe is simply overflowing with options? Maybe the problem is too much choice. Or maybe you're just bored of it all and a wardrobe refresh is what you need. After all, a few new outfits won't break the bank, and the old ones look so ragged so quickly, even if you've only worn them a few times. These days we're not expected to make them last anyway. That's the whole point of fast fashion, isn't it?

Our fashion addiction is now the second-biggest industrial polluter on the planet. Estimates vary but it could be responsible for up to a tenth of greenhouse gas emissions – more than aviation and shipping combined. By 2030, it's estimated that the global textile industry will be worth over $2 trillion. If it were a national economy, it wouldn't scrape into the top 20, and yet its carbon footprint may be on track to rival the whole of the EU's unless efforts to curb those emissions intensify dramatically.

The good news is that it's achievable – but this is a battle not just for the makers but for the wearers of clothes. It will take some effort and investment by all players.

❦

Streamlining the production of clothing has been on the agenda since the Industrial Revolution. But as new technologies and innovations began to facilitate the mass production of cloth- ing, granting more and more people access to a steady flow of fashion options, the use of oil and petrochemicals started to add up. Now, from carbon emissions to pesticides and landfill, the environmental – and human – costs of fashion are racked up at every stage of the product's life cycle, from design and manu- facture to distribution, wear and, ultimately, disposal.

Creating the fabric is an industrial process. Almost two- thirds of clothing contains synthetic fibres, essentially a form of plastic, most of which – including spandex and nylon – are derived from oil. Turning oil into fabric is energy intensive: for every tonne of polyester produced, 5 tonnes of carbon dioxide is released into the atmosphere, the equivalent of five return transatlantic flights.

Natural fabrics, meanwhile, have their own dark secret. Cotton accounts for over a third of the planet's textile demand, but while it has half the carbon footprint of synthetics, it is also the thirstiest fabric on the planet. A pair of jeans and T-shirt typically slurp up 15,000 litres of water, enough to keep the average human going for fifteen years in terms of drinking water. And cotton is often grown in countries where water is already in short supply, such as India where groundwater is diverted to feed the crop, despite almost 100 million people not having access to safe water. Then there's the pollution. Raising cotton accounts for a sixth of global pesticide use. It also uses 2.5 per cent of the planet's arable lands. Although in some ways that is actually quite efficient, providing livelihoods for 250 million people, its typical method of cultivation contributes heavily to soil degradation and erosion.

Fabric dyes also come with a cost. The first human-made chemical dye came about in 1856 by pure accident as teenager William H. Perkin washed out a test tube following a failed chemistry experiment in east London. Fascinated by how the residue stained his cleaning cloths a vivid purple, he subsequently filed a patent for what he called mauveine, and so brought cheap, mass-produced dyes to the world, making it an infinitely more colourful place.

These days, up to 9 trillion litres of water are used in the dyeing of textiles every year. The murky soup that remains is too toxic to be reused, leaving its stain on rivers and the wildlife they support. In 2017, residents of Mumbai in India were taken aback by the sight of bright-blue stray dogs roaming around, stained after a dip in a nearby river into which untreated factory waste had flowed. In time, the dogs were rinsed clean, but the fish that populated the river were not so lucky: the levels of pollution was more than ten times higher than they could survive.

Textile production as a whole is estimated to be responsible for about 20 per cent of global clean-water pollution. The average European textile-finishing company uses over 466 grams of chemicals per kilo of fabric. But production may well be outsourced to developing countries, where rules around pollution are often less strict, and factories, particularly in China, are also more likely to rely on coal or other fossil fuels for their electricity.

When it comes to greenhouse gases, management consultant McKinsey estimates that 70 per cent of fashion's emissions are derived from 'upstream' functions – the production process, the production of the fabric and the design and manufacture of the garment.

This stage has a human cost, too. The race to knock out the competition by churning out the latest trends faster and at lower prices is increasingly intense. It can lead to an unseemly bun-fight to secure the cheapest source as some retailers 'chase the needle' around the world, looking for ways to cash in and cut costs outsourcing labour to China, India, Bangladesh, Ethiopia – wherever fingers fly fastest and at the cheapest rate.

These overseas workers labour for long hours, but they do not earn what could be termed a living wage. In Ethiopia, textile factory workers' wages in 2019 were typically less than $7 (£5.75) per week, just a third of the rates paid in Bangladesh. The government made a virtue of that, hoping to divert business from higher-cost countries. In a BBC investigation, workers from those plants complained of earning insufficient to live on, unsanitary conditions and verbal abuse. One alleged that women even had their abdomens felt to check if they were pregnant.

Working conditions are frequently not just dreadful but life-threatening. In 2013, 1,138 garment workers lost their lives in the collapse of the Rana Plaza factory complex in Bangladesh; a further 2,500 were injured. While conditions have since improved – eventually, under fierce international scrutiny – the scars linger.

Once the garments are made, the environmental costs continue as products must be shipped halfway way across the world to meet our whims: from factory floor to shop floor – or, increasingly, front door. Currently transport is not as significant a part of fashion's carbon footprint as we might assume, however. Consultants at McKinsey estimate that transport accounts for just 3 per cent of fashion's emissions. That's because the vast majority of clothing is transported by ship or road – relatively cheap ways of ferrying bulky goods around, and less environmentally damaging than by air. But to quench a thirst for rapid delivery, a growing proportion is now airborne. Estimates predict that just a 3 per cent switch from shipping to air cargo could double fashion's travel footprint.

Waste is a bigger factor. The process of manufacturing is inherently wasteful: about 15 per cent of material ends up literally on the cutting room floor as pieces of a pattern are trimmed, typically destined for the bin.

So the production process is riddled with issues before the clothes even reach the shopfloor; but the industry is trying to address some of them. One way to tackle the problems in the cotton supply chain, for example, is to increase efficiencies, thereby reducing waste, water usage and pollution. Recently, a number of initiatives have started to bring together cotton farmers, textile suppliers, retailers and even policy-makers. It's Economics 101: match the buyers and sellers in a marketplace (albeit a virtual one) and you optimise the amount sold. The Better Cotton Initiative, which aims to enable the more sustainable production of cotton with less water and chemicals, now covers farmers who churn out enough cotton to make 8 billion T-shirts.

Another option is organic cotton, which doesn't use syn-thetic pesticides or fertilisers, and is a far less thirsty crop. Retailers are clamouring for more of it and there is an excess of demand: less than 5 per cent of India's cotton is organic, but that accounts for 75 per cent of global supply. The difficulty in increasing output is that many farmers in areas such as India are small-scale, the yields of organic production are far lower, and switching production methods can be pricey – and risky. To tackle those challenges, locally run cooperatives have been set up, such as the Om Organic Cotton in Odisha, India, which brought together 4,385 Fairtrade cotton farmers to enable them to receive subsidies and share the risk. As part of the Fairtrade organisation, they are also helped to explore alternative income sources for the months when cotton isn't being produced.

Ultimately, though, there will always be issues with both cot-ton and synthetic (oil-derived) production, so across the industry, the race for more ethical synthetic materials is forging ahead. This is a key part of any brand's commitment to sustainability. One option is to increase the use of recycled plastics (rPET) in clothing, to avoid bringing any new plastics into the envir-onment. At present, the most viable route towards that is via the recycling of plastic bottles, the collection of which is well developed. Sometimes that can mean innovative solutions: the burgeoning textile industry of Sri Lanka has enlisted the country's navy to help with the collection of bottles from its surrounding seas. However, a relatively low oil price can make virgin plastics a far more affordable and attractive option than recycled ones.

Another option is to recycle existing material. The difficul-ties of turning old fabrics into new has been described as the

Achilles heel of the industry. However, it's a weakness that is increasingly being addressed. The technology for recycling synthetic fabrics is at a relatively early stage but it is evolving rapidly. A number of retailers, including H&M, Inditex and Marks and Spencer, signed up to a pledge to increase the amount of recycled polyester in their products by 2025, with targets ranging from 45 to 100 per cent. The latest available data showed that only 11 per cent of companies had achieved their target. H&M is now eyeing 2030 instead. Despite the involvement of some of the more recognisable names, the amount of polyester included in the pledge accounted for just 3 per cent of the apparel market. Turning the tide on plastic, especially in the face of fashion-focused customers, may require some concerted energy.

Natural fabrics such as cotton can be recycled more easily, but the growing use of mixed fabrics (such as cotton mixed with spandex), and limitations on methods for recycling (which can sometimes damage the fibre) have not helped. And some materials that have typically been used can be recycled only once. Again, however, the major retailers are joining up with those who are pioneering the technology to create fabrics such as 'Infinna', which is created out of cotton-rich textile waste to form a material that feels and looks like cotton and can be recycled endlessly.

Given the current limitations of recycling, however, firms are also exploring other avenues. One increasingly popular option is to find new, more sustainable materials. Bio-based synthetic polymers – the technical term for materials spun out of renewable crops such as sugar cane – are growing in popularity. Lyocell, for example, is a fabric created from wood pulp from sustainable forests. It's soft to the touch, making it a ready substitute for silk or cotton, durable, breathable and very absorbent. Its production can be described as a 'closed loop' as it uses non-toxic chemicals that can be reused, and it requires less land and less dye than cotton. The overall process can take a matter of a few hours. But this wonder fabric has its drawbacks. It's biodegradable – but only if it's not mixed with other fibres. And, crucially, it's more expensive than the likes of cotton.

The industry is starting to make changes. But while the method of production can be cleaned up, that is only part of the solution in an industry that is growing at a phenomenal pace, with a huge focus on make, use, dispose. This is the linear economy: keeping the products churning out, keeping us buying, keeping profits flowing.

∽

How clothes are made is only part of the issue; the other is the sheer volume produced and purchased. Simply put, we buy too many clothes. In recent decades, globalisation has made clothing cheaper and cheaper, so of course we've bought more in response. If a T-shirt costs only £2, why not buy one in every colour (even if blush pink washes out your complexion)? Who cares if a £5 dress doesn't survive one round in the washing machine? But the impossibly low prices of these garments don't reflect the true cost of our impulse buys. Cheap fast fashion might not always be the worst culprit when it comes to the environmental footprint of an individual shirt – but on a scale of billions, the impact is extraordinary.

What once was a payday treat is a now a spontaneous splurge. The average European buys five times as much clothing as they did forty years ago. The average number of wears we get out of an item has fallen by over a third in the last twenty years alone. Where there were once four fashion seasons in a year, there are now dozens in retail land. New stock will 'drop' every few days, shop-window displays are replenished weekly, the latest looks flow from the catwalk to the high street within weeks rather than months.

The vast majority of these clothes also have a limited life – and a costly one in environmental terms. Over a quarter of clothing's carbon footprint is derived from 'downstream' activities – how we treat our clothes once we've bought them. Putting a load of washing on every two days and then drying that load can have the equivalent footprint on an annual basis as a return flight between London and Edinburgh. It also degrades the fabrics of clothes that increasingly were not made to last. Synthetic fabrics also shed fibres when washed. The Ellen MacArthur Foundation, set up by the Olympic gold medallist yachtswoman to promote sustainability, says this leads to half a million tonnes of tiny pieces of plastic being shed into the ocean every year, equal to each of us on the planet chucking in seven plastic bottles. These microplastics pollute oceans, freshwater and land. If consumed by animals, they can restrict growth and the ability to reproduce. A third of microplastics found in oceans are thought to have come from clothing.

In the USA – perhaps one of the worst culprits – some 85 per cent of clothes end up in landfill, a significant portion never even having been worn. Increasingly, we're buying online, and some of those purchases will inevitably be returned; if retailers do not have the capacity or technology to separate the defective from the simply unwanted, all of it will be sent on a fast track to landfill. Over 3 billion products are returned a year in the USA alone and one estimate suggests as much as a tenth of returns are destined for the dump. Synthetic 'plastic' clothes might take hundreds of years to decompose, releasing methane all the while.

The pressure to keep buying is intense. The rise of online shopping and loyalty schemes in the digital age has given retailers unprecedented access to data on our behaviour and tastes. The same technology that enables them to ensure goods are replenished before they're in danger of selling out also arms them with the knowledge of shopping patterns and how to lure us back to stick one more item in the virtual or real basket. They're not just feeding the appetite, they're stimulating it, 24/7.

To shrink fashion's footprint, analysts say the answer may be for consumers to choose to buy less. After all, no rational business is likely to desert the status quo if it's profitably satisfying customers' appetites.

In an ideal sustainable universe, prices would be elevated to reflect what economists call 'externalities' – the environmental and social costs that affect the welfare of others, either now or in the future. That would simply force us – or most of us – to buy less. It would reduce overconsumption, increase the welfare of those involved in production, and help to mitigate or prevent environmental damage. Prevention, after all, is better than cure. There are some smaller brands doing just this, but at prices that most people can't afford. A puffer jacket by brand Patagonia, renowned for a focus on sustainability, can cost ten times the high-street equivalent. A certain segment of the market is willing and able to pay a premium for ethical clothes, but those people are in the minority.

Higher prices would be commercial madness for most retailers. It would jeopardise their very essence: in a competitive market, retailers are under pressure to keep an eye not just on hemlines but on their profits. Ultimately, all companies have an obligation to shareholders to maximise profits. And customers, particularly in the twenty-first-century mass market, are very price sensitive. Put prices up, and we're likely not to go for that new pair of shoes – or we might head next door for a cheaper version. Our behaviour is therefore what's known as 'price elastic' when it comes to non-essential purchases. That's another way of saying that price really matters. (Couture dresses, by contrast, attract very different behaviour. Demand might even rise when their prices are put up. It's snob appeal, a badge of pride for the monied clientele.)

The sad truth is that there are jobs and livelihoods that rely on this endless supply of affordable, throwaway items. This raises a key question – and a key sticking point as our economy moves towards more sustainable practices. Imagine if we all stopped buying high-street fashion or, at least, just bought the bare minimum we'd need to survive. The biggest names in fashion would crumble. And that's not just the staff at company HQ, it's the whole supply chain, all the way from the shopfloor to warehousers and distributors to those cotton farmers and low-paid factory workers barely scraping together a living in India, Bangladesh and Ethiopia. As many as one in eight workers worldwide relies on the fashion and textiles machine for their livelihoods. In very broad terms, the industry has exported lower prices and choice to the West, and jobs and income to the East. It is those who can least afford it who might pay the greatest price.

Some argue that the whole model on which fashion retail is built needs to be upturned if we're serious about curbing emissions. Gradually we are seeing a shift to the idea of the circular economy: make, use, repurpose, recycle, reuse, for as long as possible. Resell, rent or refurbish an item and its lifespan typically increases by over 50 per cent. But it's a trend that needs to pick up pace. McKinsey says that we need to see one in five garments subject to the circular model by 2030 to be consistent with meeting the Paris targets on emissions reductions. The current figure is more like one in twenty. To get there, we need a fundamental wholescale shift away from the linear model being the norm to a circular one – change needs to come from both business and consumers.

When it comes to recycling, Brits are much better than their transatlantic friends at sending the majority of our discarded clothes off to charity shops, recycling plants and textile banks – enough to fill almost 500 Olympic-sized swimming pools every year. But that's not always a straightforward solution. Charity Oxfam estimates that 70 per cent of clothes donated globally end up in Africa; 40 per cent of that typically ends up in landfill. It's developed its own pioneering giant Wastesaver plant to ensure donated textiles are either resold or repurposed – for example as cleaning cloths. Oxfam claims to save over 7,000 tonnes of fabric from landfill every year in this way.

Some enterprising individuals have seen an opportunity to start up clothing rental services or resale sites. As the focus on sustainability has grown, those have boomed. Seven resale and rental platforms including Poshmark, Vinted and Rent the

Runway have each been valued at over \$1 billion dollars in recent years. Some of those may focus on the higher end of the market but the growth of eBay and Depop has also been steady. Of course, shopping online from these sorts of non-traditional retailers tends to mean no trying before buying; unsuitable items may be at more risk of getting dumped if returns aren't possible.

But traditional bricks and mortar retailers are getting in on the act too. Upmarket French department stores have dedicated permanent space to concessions selling vintage and second-hand clothes. British stalwart John Lewis has launched a service to hire out children's clothes.

This brings a new challenge for fashion retailers, though. If they want to participate, the clothes they stock have to be made with longevity in mind, not fall apart after a couple of washes. And they must step away from the notion that the way to make money is via the manufacturing of raw resources, and invest instead in repurposing, reselling or renting. That would mean overturning the current approach to supply chains and logistics and, crucially, no longer using growth in volume of sales as the metric of success. If these changes can be implemented in way that promotes efficiency and costs savings – to help the bottom line – then businesses can reap financial as well as environmental rewards.

A genuine circular economy would not only maximise resources, it would also cut waste and could make us more efficient and profitable as an economy, saving money for both businesses and consumers. For example, the linear economy model is plagued by overproduction. It's difficult for retailers to know what's going to sell when they place an order. Tastes change, the weather can be fickle and 40 per cent of garments typically end up being sold at a discount, to get them out of the way for the next lot. Under a circular model, however, there may be opportunity for fatter margins per garment and less exposure to competition. The emphasis would be on the unique rather than the ubiquitous. In total, the Ellen MacArthur Foundation reckons there's a $700 billion opportunity to grow the circular model from 3 per cent to 23 per cent of the global attire market by 2030.

Perhaps it's unrealistic, however, to expect the circular model to replace the linear economy entirely. In the near term the best approach could be refining the existing linear model, making it more semi-circular. Some companies have already made steps in this direction.

Retailers' excess stock, for example, is often dumped – or worse. In 2018 Burberry – Britain's biggest upmarket global fashion label – was revealed to have burned almost £30 million worth of clothing, accessories and perfume. Some £90 million of such items had been disposed of in this way over five years. There was nothing wrong with them; the company just didn't want to risk devaluing the brand by flog- ging off this excess stock at bargain-basement prices. Luxury brands are able to charge massive mark-ups because of their exclusivity. Become perceived as mass market and that 'snob appeal' is quickly diluted. Faced with an outcry once the issue was revealed, it vowed within weeks to end the practice, and donate, recycle or reuse the products in future. Burberry is far from the only designer label to burn excess stock but it was the first to commit to stopping.

Other brands have looked into tackling the amount of waste created by returns. H&M, for example, has delved into the world of virtual fittings, acknowledging that half of its customer returns are to do with fit. Online-only rival ASOS boasts that it processes 97 per cent of its returns for resale, and that the other 3 per cent is recycled or repurposed.

Ultimately, it is the biggest brands whose names crop up most in relation to pioneering initiatives (and face the most scrutiny from customers and media), and who have the spending power either to drive change or to maintain the status quo.

A Coruña, a coastal city teetering on the north-east coast of Spain, just above the Portuguese border, is where the first branch of Zara was opened by Amancio Ortega in 1975. A brand was born that within a couple of decades would become renowned for spinning catwalk style into affordable fashion in your local shopping centre, all within a couple of weeks. Today, its parent company Inditex has almost 7,000 branches around the globe, about 2,000 of them under the Zara marque. Given that Inditex sold over 1 billion items in 2016 alone, even the most efficient and well-intentioned business of that size will struggle to tread lightly, and avoid contributing to fashion's growing problem. Like many fashion companies, it's been under pressure to show how the future can be more sustainable.

Inditex's global headquarters still lie a few kilometres outside the city. As a rule, the company is media-shy, so it was rare to be allowed access. Its leafy grounds are home to a sprawling complex of buildings, some connected by tunnels. It could be mistaken for an understated Silicon Valley campus. Design, buying, cutting, even some manufacturing and shipping, take place here.

What lies within is a fascinating and somewhat overwhelming sight. Buried deep inside is a corridor, designed to look like one from any number of shopping centres in the world, set up with the retail equivalent of secret labs: fake stores where ideas and layouts are trialled before being rolled out across the world and where experiments are run to explore how packaging can be collected and stored for recycling.

Elsewhere, buyers rub shoulders with designers, who work metres away from pattern cutters and those who stitch together samples. It is an efficient system that makes it quick and easy to communicate about what works, get items into production and reduce waste.

A couple of hundred metres away, in another building, a machine cuts out the pieces for a coat, many at a time, plough-ing through a stack of material in one rhythmic move. Those components had been designed and then tessellated to minimise the material left on the cutting room floor.

Rows of identical boxes are then fed into an intricate and hypnotic conveyor track system, not dissimilar to a mini ski lift. One is headed to a Rome store; another destined for Texas. The contents of each are dictated by the real-time automated stock systems in each outlet, designed to let head office know what is selling well, what needs replenishing and what is worth repeat-ing in a different fabric in the next mini-season.

About half of Inditex's suppliers lie within a flight time of 2.5 hours – handy for turning around designs fast, keeping an eye on quality and conditions in the supply chain – and, of course, keeping that burgeoning environmental footprint under control.

Increasingly, environmentally conscious brands such as Inditex are also switching to renewable sources of energy, which could pay off – and not just in good PR – as those sources become cheaper. That could be one of the biggest carbon savings to be made under the linear model.

The brand has also committed to 'sustainable' fabrics by 2030, and at its gleaming headquarters it is keen to display its forward-looking eco credentials. In one room, displays of pellets explain how plastic bottles are refashioned into a material for a blazer, or cotton waste turned into cellulose fabrics for strappy frocks.

This huge, centralised, slick operation is geared towards efficiency and reducing costs, which in turn reduces waste and emissions. In other words, becoming greener can complement profitability. However, while the company is aiming to halve emissions by 2030 and reach net zero by 2040, like its high-street rivals it still faces accusations of encouraging over-consumption and overproduction. In the run-up to Christmas 2023, its sales were 14 per cent higher than the year before. Inditex's bosses have previously said it's not the retailer's role to deny customers choice.

Much of the change that is happening has been driven by consumer pressure. A 2020 survey by sustainability charity Fashion Revolution found that 80 per cent of consumers in Europe aged sixteen to seventy-four claimed to want to know more about how their clothes are made, to know the sustainability credentials of the item they're buying. Of course, good intentions aren't always followed by action but customer preference has the power to dictate future trends, turning what might appear to be passing fads into business as usual.

Now, no major retailer's virtual shopfront – its website – is complete without a statement of its eco credentials and goals. Green sells. Canny retailers know that there is money to be made out of seeming green, even if they are just salving a shopper's conscience. However, one of the biggest issues here is accountability. How do we know whose claims are correct? Some claims are more worthy than others. They range from the groundbreaking to outright greenwash: incomplete, mislead-ing or even nonsensical claims. Terms such as 'positive impact' or 'negative waste', 'green' or even 'eco-friendly' are bandied around without any evidence or further detail to back them up. 'Natural' can be toxic; nothing on this earth is 'chemical-free'. 'Made with recycled fabric' could refer to less than a fifth of the material in that item. 'Carbon neutral' means firms typically donate to forest restoration projects – but who's monitoring the amount and the effectiveness of that policy? If you buy food marked 'organic' or 'free range', you know what you're getting. Those definitions are tightly regulated by many governments. Not so with many of the 'sustainable' boasts touted by fashion retailers, so any such claim needs to be treated with caution. And the bigger the green claims, the bigger the potential for greenwash. Buyer, beware.

Companies know what they're doing with these marketing tactics. Research by Britain's competition watchdog found that 60 per cent of shoppers were prepared to pay a premium of up to 9 per cent for products perceived to be environmentally friendly. That watchdog is concerned enough to have launched a probe into the claims of fashion brands. It warns that there could come a point when consumers become so disillusioned with green claims that they give up on buying eco-friendly options.

Given all the potential pitfalls, many consumers simply wish to be able to make an informed choice. This should, in theory, help reduce the more unpalatable side effects of our fast-fashion habit as consumers would increasingly shun products with suspect origins.

Of course, while the perfectly competitive market – in which everyone knows what they're buying and can make fully informed decisions – may be the stalwart of economics textbooks, it fails to make the jump off the page in its entirety into real life. For a market to be truly competitive – and the bad players weeded out – buyers should have complete access to accurate information on the product. That means not just knowing whether the claims on the tags are correct – i.e., is it really a Burberry coat? Made of wool? – but also what's not on there. That includes any of the other relevant information that is becoming increasingly important to consumers: the carbon footprint, for example, or the conditions under which it is made.

The difficulty for consumers – and retailers too for that matter – is that it's impossible to measure the carbon footprint of fashion without full transparency of the supply chain. The fashion industry spun its threads around the world, creating a global network of supply and demand. Untangling those threads is now no easy task. Retailers are, for the most part, literally shopfronts for often highly intricate supply chains. Just as a smartphone is made up of dozens of components from multiple countries, so too is the average pair of jeans, and there is a huge range of different factors to take into consideration, as we've seen, from water use and pollution to chemical consumption and waste management. In some cases, the retailer owns or tightly controls the suppliers and factories (known as vertical integration). It's a handy way of keeping a close eye on production costs, streamlining processes and cutting down on delays. But, by and large, with the need for flexibility and keeping costs down, companies have an arm's-length relationship with suppliers.

As a result, the unethical wool can be pulled over retailers' keen eyes too. It's often very difficult to be certain that suppliers are using the recycled materials they claim, for example, or reducing pesticide use. There are codes of conduct, agreed standards and spot checks to keep track, and the threat of a contract being ripped up if those terms are not met. But however well intentioned and diligent retailers might be, the reality is that they might not be able to keep a close eye on what goes on in every nook of every factory or field across the globe.

There have been incidents of organic cotton fraud in the wider industry, and a fifth of the world's cotton comes from China's Xinjiang province, an area where reports claim over half a million Uyghur Muslims have been forced to toil in the fields. That has made many organisations (including the Better Cotton Initiative) pull out or rethink their supplies from that region.

Even the Better Cotton programme doesn't promise traceability, as the cotton is often mixed with other, conventionally produced fibres. The rationale is that producing a bigger volume via what the Initiative calls 'mass balance' keeps costs down to attract consumers. But ultimately users don't know the type of cotton they're getting.

Elsewhere, a few years ago, some Zara customers in Turkey found notes in clothes from garment workers claiming they hadn't been paid and asking for them to push for better labour standards. The clothes had been made by a third-party supplier,

Textil Baskstil. Zara blamed the situation on the sudden closure of the factory and disappearance of its owner, and said it was setting up a hardship fund to compensate workers.

Apps such as Good on You are among the resources that pledge to scour a range of data points to rate brands on their impact on the environment, people and animals, helping customers to make informed choices. Some brands themselves are seeking credibility from such third-party programmes. But shoppers need to keep a careful eye on the label there too. For example, many brands have signed up to the independent Carbon Disclosure Project, which grades environmental performance. However, they may score as having reduced emissions even if the total amount they produce has gone up, as long as that's outpaced by their revenue. They're being rewarded ultimately for growth – and that's a fundamental problem.

Some of the most exciting changes have been happening in smaller brands, where traceability across supply chains is easier, and at grassroots level. Swedish denim label Amendi's products come with 'Fabrication Facts' labels, which, reminiscent of nutritional labels, detail everything from energy and water usage to a cost breakdown across the supply chain. Having a small range and close relationships with only a handful of suppliers helps.

Clothing suppliers say in a few years we could be nearing a point where it will be possible to replicate what small brands like Amendi are doing: make an approximation of the carbon footprint of a garment and add that to the label on a far wider scale. At the moment, however, we largely have to take most companies' word for it. Consumers are presented with a dazzling array of choice from a complex market with opaque supply chains.

ဢ

How fashion's 'externalities' are tackled – from recognising them, to deciding who bears responsibility, how they're incentivised to take action and who picks up the tab – will determine how successful we are in curbing harm to the planet's resources. Consumers and businesses have taken steps in the right direction, but there are limitations, as we've seen. To carry on at speed, the industry might need a legislative push.

The state is meant to get to the parts the commercial world won't or can't change. While most countries of course already have laws the industry must abide by (preventing, say, the discharging of harmful chemicals into waterways), regulating the ethical impact of our clothes has largely been left to the retailer and the free market to deal with. Given that the lure of new eco-conscious markets, conscience or peer pressure isn't always enough to prompt businesses to change their practices, governments have a role to nudge behaviour through incentives or penalties.

So, what might governments be able to do to reduce the negative effects of fast fashion, while balancing all of the economic and social issues? One option is to regulate or offer assistance via subsidies, or create networks to share best practice and know-how, along the lines of the Institute of Positive Fashion. Or they can introduce taxes to try to incorporate (some) of the real social and environmental costs in the price tag. The basic idea is to level the playing field to give sustainable production a leg up so it can compete with what is still the overriding model: offshore sourcing and less environmentally friendly materials.

Suggestions have included taxing not just the use of virgin plastics but also any synthetic garment that contains less than 50 per cent recycled plastic. A government might work with retailers to improve traceability in the supply chain via the use of digital technology to ensure environmental and labour standards are being adhered to. It could create an investment fund to aid the development of recycled fabrics and those made from sustainable crops.

If garment disposal is causing such a problem, how about banning the burning of fabrics that could be reused or recycled, and also their depositing in landfill sites? When Burberry committed to stop burning its excess stock, that was because as a FTSE 100 company, the information was published in its annual report, and widely scrutinised. It is far easier for smaller or privately owned enterprises to keep such practices going without exposure, so regulation could help.

Why not go further and levy a small charge on producers to help fund the sorting, collecting and recycling of clothes, which is already being done in France? In the UK, it's estimated that even a penny added onto every garment sold in the UK would raise £35 million per year. Greater tax breaks could be given to those donating clothes to charity for resale. VAT could be lowered on clothing repair services to encourage the extension of an item's lifestyle. Why not mandate lessons in how to repair clothing for schoolchildren, establish the habit of make do and mend early in life? Governments could also bring together water companies, washing-machine manufacturers and retailers to tackle the thorny issue of fibres being shed in the weekly laundry and finding their way into oceans.

Such practical recommendations were among those made by the UK parliament's Environmental Audit Committee in 2019. Its report claimed that the major retailers they'd spoken to weren't doing enough to clean up their act. The government, however, opted not to take up these proposals, claiming its policies were already aligned with what the committee wanted to achieve. Beyond a Plastic Packaging Tax that came into force in 2022 and an intention to look at the marine impact of microfibre shedding, it chose to let the industry sign up for voluntary measures.

The UK government is far from the only one unwilling to put taxes in place that would be blamed for undermining the high street, making a deeper hole in the pockets of consumers, as well as costing thousands of jobs. It's profit versus planet, and calculating the social cost of a decision can be tricky.

There can also be downsides to well-intentioned regulation. The Rana Plaza tragedy in Bangladesh was followed – eventually, after several years – by improvements in working and safety standards. But someone had to pay the price, and widespread protests five years later revealed it had led to lower wages. The cost of complying with tougher safety rules had been passed on to the already poorly paid workers, while the price being paid to suppliers in this competitive market had also declined, according to one consultant.

Equally, bringing production back home could reduce the carbon footprint, speed up supply and create jobs, ticking many boxes for the fast-fashion sector in particular. But that doesn't always equal ethical either. A small number of operations in Leicester, one of the UK's main textiles centres, have been found to be breaching conditions from pay to safety and working hours.

While the circular economy might seem like a simple concept, getting there is much harder. The industry is already making some tweaks, its carbon footprint growing less quickly than the volume of garments it's pumping out. But, ultimately, it's still on track to miss its 2030 targets, which were set in line with the Paris Agreement. In fact, without more concerted efforts, some estimates say its emissions could be more than double the target.

Bringing the concept of the circular economy out of the margins, making it the norm, a point of pride, would radically change that direction. Ultimately, at the consumer level our obsession with newness needs to change. We need to embrace being out of fashion to make the industry green, and reduce our purchases by about half.

In a few years' time, when we make the daily trek to our wardrobes, they might feel a lot emptier, the fabrics a little different. The dilemma over what to wear might be less onerous too.

3

Checking Your Phone

Protecting the rare resources
consumed by technology

You pick up your smartphone to check your work messages. You used to wait until you were in the office, but all this technology lets you stay plugged in all day every day from multiple devices, blurring the lines between home and work. Although this phone does seem to be slowing down a bit. And the battery isn't that great any more. It's over a year old, you realise; maybe it's time to upgrade to the latest model and throw this one to the back of the drawer with the rest of them in their little outdated-tech graveyard.

Embrace it, fear it or resist its march, technology is vital in our twenty-first-century life.

We're on our phones all the time. They hold our emails, our messages, our photos, our shopping lists, the maps that

§

show us where to go and how to get there, the calendar to plan our days. Sometimes we even make calls on them. And they're by no means the only bit of gadgetry we're hooked on: there are also laptops, desktop computers, tablets, smartwatches, flatscreen TVs.

There are over 7 billion mobile phones on the planet, and over 6 billion of those are smartphones. That's enough for 85 per cent of the world's population, although, in reality, some needy souls own more than one. Four out of five Germans have at least one handset, as do three out of four Americans, but only one in four Pakistanis. Unsurprisingly, perhaps, smartphone ownership is highest among the under-thirties.

Most people upgrade their phones every two to three years. That's about the time the battery starts to slow down. While items like our laptops and tablets tend to last a bit longer, it's estimated that they are replaced on average every three to five years too. That's an awful lot of technology for an awful lot of people being replaced at a pretty rapid rate. The amount discarded each year outweighs the Great Wall of China, according to the World Economic Forum – over 50 million tonnes, or more than 7 kilograms for each person on the planet.

Compared with other industries, all these electronics might not contribute as heavily to global emissions – somewhere between 1.5 per cent and 6 per cent – but that isn't the only impact they have. Given the vast numbers bought and discarded every year, there is a huge amount of waste in the tech industry, particularly considering how many resources go into the making of each gadget.

The production of a smartphone accounts for the largest part of its carbon footprint. Whatever brand takes your fancy (or fits your budget), the basics are the same, containing a brain-scrambling list of components and materials. It requires an LCD screen, microphone, speakers, camera, battery, rear cover – and that's before you even get to the circuit board, which puts the smart into smartphones. Plastic, silicon, iron, nickel, copper, tin . . . the list seems endless. One study suggests an iPhone necessitates 200 suppliers. The *New York Times* claims its manufacture has 400 stages and almost 100 production lines. It's a vastly complex supply chain.

Some of the materials involved are now in very high demand. This is partly because they are also fast becoming bedrocks of the green transition due to their use in items such as rechargeable batteries and wind turbines. But they have a significant environmental and human cost. And as with many industrial products, reducing that environmental impact is not straightforward.

Lithium, for example, is used in all sorts of batteries, from 2–3 grams in a mobile phone battery, to around 5 grams in a laptop battery and up to 12 kilograms in a Tesla battery. As our demand for all these different types of tech has soared, so too has the appetite for lithium. In Chile and Bolivia, it tends to be found in dried lake beds. Extracting it means drilling into those salt flats, then pumping brine to the surface to evaporate. For each tonne of lithium, the process uses 2 million litres of water, a precious resource in some of the driest landscapes in the world, displacing local farmers. It also involves toxic chemicals that can poison the remaining water supply. In 2016, a toxic leak from a lithium mine in Upper Tibet led to dead fish washing up on the banks of a nearby river; fish that nearby residents flung onto the streets in protests that temporarily stopped pro-duction. Hard-rock mining is an alternative way of sourcing lithium elsewhere, but it is more carbon intensive, and also involves the use of toxic chemicals.

Cobalt too has been in hot demand for battery production. The brittle, silvery-blue metal takes its name from the medieval German word for 'goblin' because early miners feared that it produced toxic vapours. Its modern provenance can be just as sinister. Its extraction is damaging to the environment, polluting water and damaging crops. About a fifth of cobalt comes from small, informal and unregulated mines in the Democratic Republic of the Congo (DRC). Investigations by organisations such as Amnesty International and UNICEF have found the use of child labour is common, and one report suggested as many as 40,000 people were working in unsanitary, cramped and dangerous conditions to get at this precious commodity.

Cobalt from mines such as these can leach into the supply chain via a centralised global commodities market and distri-bution system and via large refineries, often in China, making it hard to trace its origins. In 2019, a landmark legal case was launched against the world's largest tech companies, including Apple and Google, by Congolese families who said their chil-dren had been killed or injured while working illegally at mines owned by the UK mining giant Glencore. Their harvest was sold on to an intermediary, a metal and mining trader, which then sold on the battery-grade cobalt to the tech giants. Regardless of the brand, it can be hard to know how ethical the latest models of mobile phones are.

There aren't many alternative sources. Cobalt mining is

gathering pace in Australia, where it is extracted as a by-product of carbon and nickel. But the fossil fuels involved can give that process a far higher carbon footprint.

Our gadgets also use one of the most contested groups of metals: rare earths. They're embedded in modern life – from our gadgets to missile defence systems and wind turbines – and they are set to become increasingly so. They have been included on the US Geological Survey list of fifty minerals critical for the USA's national security and economy.

Rare-earth metals are a group of seventeen metallic elements, described as 'iron grey to silvery lustrous metals' that are 'typically soft, malleable, and ductile; and usually reactive' by the US Geological Survey. Cerium, terbium, neodymium . . . they languish in the lesser explored corners of the periodic table, and the Earth's crust.

Unlike many other ores, rare earths are distributed relatively consistently across the planet. They are called 'rare' not because they are scarce but because the extraction process is expensive – and toxic. For example, they're sometimes found in minerals that also contain uranium. If the pure ore needs to be extracted from radioactive materials, that process requires huge amounts of chemicals that are carcinogenic toxins, such as sulphates and hydrochloric acid. Processing one tonne of rare earths produces nearly 2,000 tonnes of toxic waste. And a vast amount of energy is needed.

Who would take on such a job? Attracted by the increasingly coveted prize at the end, China invested heavily in mining and processing from the mid-1980s. In 1992, then leader Deng Xiaoping said: 'The Middle East has oil; China has rare earths.' By 2015, it supplied 85 per cent of the world's rare-earth metals.

But much of the explosion in extraction and refining was enacted without sufficient environmental safeguards.

Nowhere bears the scars of that as much as Baotou, the source of more than half of China's rare-earths output. The city lies some 650 kilometres north-west of Beijing, in China's Inner Mongolia Autonomous Region. It's been described as one of the country's frontier towns, the population exploding from 100,000 in the 1950s to over 2.5 million today, with hastily flung-up apartment blocks and plants nestling among pipes and choked highways. Most of the rare earths processed here are extracted in the Bayan Obo mining area in the Gobi Desert, where the largest open-pit mine spans 50 kilometres. It's 130 kilometres north of Baotou but its impact is felt close to home.

The huge amount of toxic waste produced in processing rare earths means Baotou's industry chugs out around 10 million tonnes of wastewater per year. It's pumped into waterways not far from the city centre, creating toxic rivers. Crops and animals have perished alongside crusty pools of radioactive black sludge; residents who can't move away have seen growing rates of cancers of the pancreas and lungs, and leukaemia. The air has been clogged with coal dust and vapours of sulphuric acid. China's own people have paid a heavy price for its determination to corner the markets in the twenty-first-century manufacturing race, and it means that even some components of 'clean' energy have very grimy beginnings. While some improvements have been made, many of the problems remain.

We're reliant on these rare earths now. No matter the cost to the environment and human life, those mines are in little danger of becoming stranded assets. There has been minimal external pressure to clean up the process, if indeed that is even possible. But interest in doing so is growing, as countries realise the potential dangers of becoming so reliant on a single – and somewhat temperamental – source of supply.

Around the globe, countries and companies became hooked on the stream of affordable rare earths flowing out of China. Then, in 2007, China began restricting and taxing its rare-earths exports, allegedly to improve its environmental record. The move prompted an outcry from its largest foreign customers: Japan, the USA and the EU, who saw it as no more than a cynical move to drive up prices – which quadrupled – and hold the world to ransom.

About a decade later, China threatened to restrict its sale of these elements once again to the USA, weaponising them in an escalating trade war. A 2018 report from the US Department of Defense claimed that China 'strategically flooded the global market' with rare earths at cheaper prices to drive out and deter current and future competitors. If the bumpy relations between Washington and Beijing weren't already raising concerns over the USA's ability to maintain access to these metals, then the slowing of their production with the onset of the Covid-19 pandemic in 2020 heightened concerns over security of supply. But with few alternatives to these elements, China held the trump card.

The arrival of the Biden administration in 2021 heralded a renewed emphasis on – and investment in – climate change technology while tackling the national security threat posed by China. Within a month of occupying the White House, the new president had signed an executive order to review gaps in the domestic supply chain for rare earths, chips and other key resources. This was followed with a $30 million initiative to tap into researching and securing the US domestic supply chain for rare earths and other minerals used in battery-making.

But determination and a multi-million-dollar cheque do not mean the problem's solved. Sourcing rare earths in sufficient amounts cleanly has not been viable in the USA before, and the dangers remain far from eliminated. The USA once dominated the processing of rare-earth metals, after the discovery of high concentrations of metals on Mountain Pass in California in the late 1940s. Given the growing use of rare earths in techno-logical advancements such as colour television sets, medical scanners, lasers and microchips, Mountain Pass and its contents were in high demand until 1997, when the company behind the mine found itself in legal strife. Leaks from wastewater pipes were found to have contaminated the Mojave National Preserve with trace amounts of radioactive materials, and the mine closed. It was snapped up by a new buyer but it sank into bankruptcy in 2014.

It was bought again in 2017 by a company with ambitions to get rare-earth mining and processing back on US soil in the next few years, but the economics of the industry are not straightforward. The pressure is on for the USA to quickly scale up not just the mining of these resources but the processing and refining of them without detriment to the environment, and at the same time to compete on cost with China. It's a tall order. Hopes were also raised in January 2023 when a government-backed mining company in Sweden announced the discovery of around 1 million tonnes of rare-earth metals, Europe's biggest such deposit. But this is no quick fix either: the company has said that production would take ten to fifteen years and that the oxides exist in low concentrations, which means it will have to navigate the costs of extraction and building the appropriate processing centres.

In the meantime, China can continue to call the shots on the supply of rare earths, and on the environmental impact of their production. It remains to be seen if it is able and willing to clean up its act.

China hasn't just cornered the market in terms of the materials, it also manufactures most of our electronics. In 2021 around two-thirds of mobile phones were produced there, while India accounted for one in six handsets and Vietnam one in ten. But China's global dominance in manufacturing has come at a steep cost. It is by far the biggest emitter of carbon dioxide, producing over 11 megatonnes per year. That's as much as the USA, EU and India combined. That's mostly because of the energy needed for manufacture on this scale, and where that energy comes from.

Despite China being the world leader in developing and installing renewables such as wind and solar, 60 per cent of its energy still comes from coal. It burns more than the rest of the world put together, and officials continue to greenlight new plants, despite the consequences being literally right in front of their faces.

In November 2021, as the final touches were being put on the plans for the Winter Olympics in Beijing, aspiring athletes across China's capital were called back inside. Schools were ordered to shut playgrounds and cancel PE lessons, and highways were closed as smog levels spiked, bringing visibility down to less than 200 metres.

Beijing is no stranger to smog but attempts by authorities to bring down emissions levels had made such episodes less frequent. The official line was 'unfavourable weather conditions and regional pollution spread'. But it didn't take much to see beyond the narrative smokescreen.

China relies on imports for its oil and gas, so its coal supply is important to keep the lights on. In 2021, as the world tried to fire up its production lines in the aftermath of lockdowns, natural gas shortages had forced power cuts and factory closures, prompting the authorities to stoke the coal furnaces even more to fill in the gaps. In August 2021 the Chinese government had approved forty-three new coal-fired generators for domestic use. The return of severely clogged, choking air conditions was a sensory reminder of how China's economic realities can clash with its environmental goals.

In November 2021, as the residents of Beijing were battling their way through smog, world leaders and their negotiating teams were gathering thousands of kilometres away in Glasgow on the west coast of Scotland for COP 26. The aim of the environmental conference was to wrestle over how to meet the ambitions of the agreement struck in Paris in 2015 to limit global warming to 1.5–2°C. But the Conference of the Parties was being conducted without the biggest party of them all. Chinese President Xi Jinping declined to turn up to the summit in person – a move hailed as a 'big mistake' by President Biden. 'The fact that China is trying to assert, understandably, a new role in the world as a world leader – not showing up – come on!' He exclaimed.

And foot-dragging by the members of the Chinese delegation who were there and Indian negotiators led to a notably delayed and watered-down final statement from the summit, crucially resulting in a pledge to 'phase down' rather than 'phase out' the use of coal. Without the wholehearted commitment of the biggest polluters, it left the ability to hit the Paris targets on a knife-edge and the UK's COP 26 lead, Alok Sharma, a seasoned politician, publicly on the verge of tears.

But there has been progress since. Under the Sunnylands deal, arrived at in late 2023 (and named for the Californian estate where the special envoys from each nation met), the USA and China agreed on 'accelerating renewable energy deployment in their respective economies'. It admittedly omitted explicit targets to reduce coal emissions, and the language around fossil fuels as a whole remained a little vague. For the first time, China – the world's largest emitter of greenhouse gas – outlined specific actions to curb methane emissions, which arise mainly from coal. It at least hinted at a shift in mindset.

Other countries might criticise China's reluctance to give up its coal but in its quest for development and a more prosperous existence for its population, it is proceeding along the well-trodden path of industrialisation, leading to higher emissions, which so many other nations have already gone down.

China has pointed out that actually, if you look back over time, the USA is the biggest instigator of climate change. Since 1750, according to respected website Our World in Data, the USA has produced over 400 billion tonnes of carbon dioxide. China, by contrast, has emitted only half as much, and most of that within the last fifty years or so.

In recent years, however, the US has seen emissions peak and then fall as it shifts away from coal, and renewable options increase. While the USA accounted for around 13 per cent of emissions in 2019 (admittedly still punching way above its weight, with just 4 per cent of the world's population), China accounted for 30 per cent.

This process can be explained by an economic theory called the environmental Kuznets curve, which is a way of looking at changes in income alongside environmental emissions. Essentially, it describes a trade-off between income and environmental degradation.

The environment often suffers in the early stages of industrial development. However, after a certain level of economic growth – or so the theory goes – a society can more easily afford to re-establish its relationship with the environment.

This can happen for a combination of reasons. Take the UK, for example. Direct emissions from the UK apparently peaked in 1972. But that's largely because an increasing proportion of the goods used in the UK were manufactured abroad. Those emissions were 'exported' to the areas where the items were made (principally China, followed by the EU). Take those 'exported' emissions into account, and domestic carbon dioxide emissions didn't peak until 2007. After that, a greater push on environmental policies, coupled with more investment in areas such as cleaner energy and energy-efficient production and transport, helped drive down the UK's directly produced emissions. That was aided by an increasing dependence (typical in advanced economies) on a less carbon-intensive service sector, and a shift away from a more polluting manufacturing one.

So, in theory, the environmental Kuznets curve should resemble a bell: after an initial surge in emissions – because this kind of economic growth is typically emission heavy – a plateau is reached before pollution starts to come down.

Is decarbonisation then the luxury of the affluent, the early adopters of industrial revolution, who can now afford to go for greener options without compromising basic standards of living for their citizens? After all, countries such as China and India are aiming for their people to enjoy what those in the West typically already do: higher incomes and rising standards of living through economic development. Is it fair to deny developing countries the chance to do the same?

However, the journey away from heavy emissions is not inevitable; it takes the combined will of many people, governments, consumers and businesses. What if they're committed instead to maintaining growth at the lowest financial cost, regardless of the environmental one, even as people become wealthier? Then the curve gets distorted – and some fear that China could be a prime example of this. The Sunnylands agreement gives new hope that this scenario won't come to pass, that China is now pursuing a more concentrated version of the development process experienced in the West: seeking growth while also decarbonising. Whether that happens remains to be seen. In the meantime, China's net zero target of 2060 remains less ambitious than that of many other nations, including the USA, and analysts reckon it will require trillions of dollars more investment. Plus it has to align that with its growth aims.

The conflict between carbon neutrality and energy security is a difficult sum to square. China won't reach the former goal without peeling away from coal – yet it has more reserves of that fuel than any other nation, and it may be a hard habit to break for such a vast industrial giant. Yet China's rapid investment in green technology is paying off – fast. For the first time, the country's renewable capacity (largely wind, solar and hydro) accounted for half of its total generation capacity in 2023, out-stripping coal, according to its state media agency. China has a long way to go but that progress is at least encouraging.

Global consumers might baulk at the fact that our gadgets are derived from such a filthy power source but, at this point, alternatives are limited. Phone companies have been looking to diversify, not least due to concerns about security issues when it comes to China and in the face of the wake-up call provided by the pandemic, when China's production lines slowed drastically amid shutdowns. Foxconn, maker of iPhones, is eyeing expansion in India, but that country relies on coal for half its energy; it's hardly a vast improvement. Even if the odd phone factory shifts elsewhere, it will take a lot to unseat China from its position as the manufacturing powerhouse of the world economy.

Phones, tablets, games consoles, laptops . . . our gadgets have become an intrinsic part of our lifestyle. To feed our addic-tions, we've become reliant on producers that can keep up with the latest model at an affordable price tag. But that lower cost might mean relying on countries that are yet to catch up on the green transition – either out of necessity or to feed their economic ambitions.

§

Technology could well be a driving force of the green revo-lution. After all, a smartphone makes us more efficient and can reduce our carbon footprint in several ways. It enables groceries to arrive on your doorstep at the touch of a button, for example, cutting out a drive to the shops. But that doesn't compensate for the environmental impact of the gadget itself.

Few of us would be prepared to undergo a permanent digital detox, even if it means putting up with a dirty footprint. There are other ways, however, of cleaning up that footprint while we wait for the industry to find ways to be greener. Making our gadgets last as long as possible is the obvious answer – looking after them, getting them fixed rather than moving on at the first sign of trouble or the launch of a shiny new version.

However, realistically, gadgets do break, and those batteries do degrade. Then the most important thing is what we do with the old ones. Many of us simply contribute to the growing pile of e-waste. As many as 5 billion handsets may be at risk of being thrown out per year, the majority headed perhaps for landfill where they may pollute the soil, their less palatable ingredients leaching into waterways. Many more will be flung to the back of a drawer, joining a whole host of other discarded electronics. That might seem a better option, but that still means that all those valuable resources that went into the phone – metals, plastics, those rare earths – are going to waste when they could be extracted and reused. Properly recycling all of our old gadgets could have a huge impact.

This is where companies have a role to play in encouraging their customers to change their habits. Many mobile phone networks and retailers operate trade-in schemes, allowing you to cash in and the phone to be refurbished and resold or recycled for parts. Some also have a no-landfill waste pledge.

There are other ways companies can look at the environmental impact of their products, though, at the design and manufacture stages. Increasing the charging efficiency, for example, reduces the amount of power a gadget uses over its lifetime. Standardising chargers across all makes and models – as indeed, the EU is mandating – is intended to cut down on the amount of e-waste. And many companies are looking at using as much recycled materials in their new products as possible. Apple, for example, claims 20 per cent of the materials in its iPhone are recycled, including nearly all of the rare-earth elements.

Ideally, it could be argued, they could further help by not putting temptation our way, and bringing out the latest models less frequently. After all, the average upgrade is hardly life-changing. But companies exist to make a profit and, just like the fashion giants, their role is to cater to our taste, the clamour for newness. It doesn't make business sense to do anything else. Ultimately, the decision to upgrade lies in the hands of consumers themselves. The group most likely to own a smartphone – the under-thirties – are also the ones reportedly the most passionate about change. They could hold the key for persuading companies to take the right steps. For now, though, there is a long way to go to make the global explosion in consumer technology sustainable.

4

Receiving a Parcel

Untangling the complex web of the global shipping network

There's the doorbell; the package you ordered just yesterday afternoon is here already. You've got to give it to them, they're quick. It's all so convenient and you order so much online these days that the courier's face has become a more familiar sight than your neighbour's. Many of us have become accustomed to an Amazon Prime lifestyle, the one where you click and a package will magically turn up on your doorstep the very next day, or maybe even the same one. But when you place an order, how often are you thinking that it might come with a side order of . . . oil?

It doesn't matter if the item was from a retailer just a couple of kilometres down the road, it was probably manufactured abroad. It will then have been shipped to the port, unloaded at the other end, whisked off to a distribution centre and then dispatched to the final destination: a long journey involving freight forwarders, warehousing groups and last-mile delivery couriers. Every leg of that package's journey is likely to have been powered by oil – heavy shipping fuel or light, sweet gasoline – belching out carbon as well as a multitude of other greenhouse gases and noxious substances.

At the moment, around 100 million barrels of oil are consumed every day. Oil is used in everything from the manufacture of vehicles and fuel to the maintenance of the roads and in the creation of an infinite number of products we use in our daily lives: nail varnish, the coating on TV screens, floor wax, antihistamines, dyes, dishwasher parts, even life jackets. If we're to meet Paris emission targets, we're going to have to cut our consumption by the equivalent of one in three barrels of oil by 2050. That's going to require a huge transformation of the vast global trading and shipping network that feeds the consumer lifestyle we've become accustomed to.

❧

The amount of stuff transported around the globe on board ships has quadrupled over the last forty years to quench our thirst for consumption, to feed the expanding world economy. Eleven billion tonnes of cargo crosses the seas per year. That's about 1.5 tonnes per person on average, about thirty times their body weight. These goods are transported at a relatively low financial cost. The industry reckons that shipping accounts for less than a tenth of the price of a cup of coffee, $5 of a $100 pair of trainers. But what of the hidden cost?

Some 90 per cent of the world's cross-border trade in goods is carried out by sea; it's the quiet mainstay of global trade. It is also its dirty secret. Pre-pandemic, more than 90,000 ships criss-crossed oceans. Between them, they combusted almost 2 billion barrels of fuel every year, using the heaviest type of oil, the filthy dregs, derived from a barrel of crude. The shipping trade is responsible for creating 3 per cent of the world's total human-made greenhouse gas emissions – all to cater for our growing demands and whims. By 2050, without action, that could double. Heavy shipping fuel also gives rise to pollutants such as sulphur dioxide, nitrogen oxides and particulate matter. Those most vulnerable to its impacts aren't the recipients of the cargo but those living closest to the coasts that line the busiest shipping routes, often in developing nations. The biggest culprit is the lane running from Asia to Europe. Belching ocean-going vessels are calculated to account for one in six of the 400,000 or so premature deaths globally linked to air pollution, claims a 2019 study from the International Council on Clean Transportation.

In Chapter 1 we saw how energy transitions occur and how power generation has gradually been getting cleaner – in the West, at least. But when it comes to shipping and transport, oil is a bit more sticky; it seems it's harder to remove it from our lives. Of every hundred barrels, around a quarter is destined for industrial use, in manufacturing, while fewer than five are now used in the home or commercial properties for power purposes. Meanwhile, about two-thirds of those hundred barrels are destined for use in transportation.

Steps are being taken to tackle that consumption in certain areas. Electric vehicles, for example, are being scaled out around the world (see Chapter 5), but electricity cannot solve the problem across the entire sector. Oil is far more energy dense than even the most state-of-the-art battery. Put it this way: on a full tank of petrol a car might travel over 500 kilometres; a battery of the same weight might take an EV less than 40 kilometres (those batteries are usually around ten times heavier to account for that).

That's to power the average car. The heavier a vehicle is, the more energy it requires; a truck cab, for example, can be about seven times heavier than the average car before you even account for the weight of the goods it's hauling.

Given these weight issues, there are a number of areas that can't easily be electrified, mainly because the batteries can't hold enough power. Shipping, aviation and long-haul transportation all need a different fuel source in order to get away from oil, one that can compete on price and availability.

∽

Oil's typical affordability – and efficacy – has long been part of its attraction, as we saw in Chapter 1. Our infrastructure was built around it, nurturing a dependence that would become our vulnerability. Even when the price of oil goes up, we can't just stop using it altogether, and that is particularly true of global transportation, which guzzles so much of it with so few alternatives.

As oil was increasingly embedded in every aspect of our lives, it wasn't long before it became part of a very modern phenomenon: the commodities supercycle. A grand sweeping term, this typically refers to a period of anything between ten and thirty-five years where we see a surge in prices of essential commodities such as corn, copper – or oil. These cycles tend to be associated with emphatic economic upswings on a global scale, usually propelled by an overwhelming structural change to the economy. The starkest examples are the surge in industrialisation in the USA in the 1880s (to which the discovery of oil contributed), the recovery from the Great Depression in the interwar years or the explosion of industrialisation in China in the 1990s. All of these profoundly affected the way the world economy works, and resulted in an increase in demand for raw materials, including energy sources.

Prices surge at these points because when there is a rise in demand for natural resources, it is often difficult for producers to respond quickly; their supply is said to be inelastic. Shortages and bottlenecks occur. Consequently, prices tend to respond sharply, at least in the short term.

The spike in oil prices in 2022 reflected huge global demand after the Covid-19 pandemic, for example, and not enough supply, a problem that was already bad but made worse by the war in Ukraine, which heightened fears about the security of supply. Some analysts queried if we were in another supercycle. But the rise was short-lived; as concerns eased, so did the price – evidence that much of the commodities market is driven by speculation and sentiment rather than actual physical demand.

Over time, the price of oil has increasingly been determined not by OPEC fiddling with supply but by speculation – traders who will never physically see the stuff they're peddling, operating thousands of kilometres away. Unlike those using the oil, these buyers will never take delivery of a physical barrel. However, they now account for the majority of the market.

They're in it, as with many commodity traders, for a fast buck; if the exchanges are their casino, crude is their blackjack. They are betting on current and future demand.

When the price does spike, however, that encourages more production and more investment in the long term to meet demand. For example, there had been a decades-long decline in US oil production after its peak in the 1970s. There was no shortage of oil, but the easiest stores had been depleted and the technology to extract oil from unyielding shale rocks had become more difficult and expensive. However, after the oil-price shocks, shale extraction processes became financially viable. The USA is now the world's biggest oil-producing nation once again.

Of course, given the volatility in oil prices, and how sensitive they are to geopolitical shocks, this also works both ways. Any dive in the value of black gold also acts as a catalyst for these companies to address the future viability of oil. The lower the price, the harder it is to pump at a profit.

As things currently stand, it looks as though many investors and energy companies are still confident for the future of oil over the coming decades. While some energy suppliers may be gradually weaning themselves off oil, surging demand in the petrochemical and aviation sectors means that global demand overall is increasing. In a 2021 poll, about half of investors deemed big fossil fuel providers were still 'investible', their profits having just been boosted from another rise in oil prices. They do have a point: rising demand from the emerging giants – China, India – and the enthusiasm with which some consumers are clinging to their petrol cars means we may have more years of demand growth.

Take ExxonMobil, the direct descendant of John D. Rockefeller's nineteenth-century Standard Oil operation. In 2020 it saw $20 billion of assets written off and a plunge in reserves. Yet it plans to boost oil and gas production, to take advantage of what it sees as a bulge in demand in the next two decades of 16 million barrels per day – as much as the USA currently produces in total.

It's not just Exxon. After the Deepwater Horizon disaster of 2010, when a catastrophic spill on a rig pumped the equivalent of 300 Olympic swimming pools of unrefined crude into the Gulf of Mexico, BP vowed to cut oil and gas production by 40 per cent compared to 2009 levels, and to stop exploration in new countries. However, this will still mean it operates in dozens of countries, and, despite its growing commitment to renewables (see Chapter 1), its chief executive admitted hydrocarbons will be part of its identity for decades to come. High oil prices will be beneficial as it sells existing fields to other companies in order to meet its own emissions targets.

The spike in oil and gas prices in 2022 that prompted record profits for fossil fuel majors convinced many of them that our addiction to their products was far from over. It also left them with plenty of cash for future fossil fuel investment, even as they put more into developing alternative fuels. There was, they saw, going to be demand for oil and gas for some time. Indeed, while some richer countries try to cut back, governments around the world are still heavily subsidising oil to promote economic development and maintain stable economies.

And there are decades left of the stuff – if we want it.

⸎

'Just stop oil,' plead the protesters. But when it comes to shipping and transportation, what are the alternatives? And why haven't they been deemed viable wholesale replacements?

Liquid natural gas (LNG) is seen as one of the most practical alternatives. The gas is cooled and then transported by sea to its destination, rather than having to rely on access to a network of pipes. It's become more in demand generally as countries such as China try to make the switch from coal to clean up their air. The shipping industry has also embraced it, with some companies spending billions adapting their vessels to run on LNG instead of oil. Although fewer than 4 per cent of vessels on the sea in 2023 were LNG ready or capable of being easily adapted, almost 30 per cent of those on order were.

As we've seen, however, while gas does produce fewer emissions than coal, it's hardly clean energy. LNG is made up of methane, a gas eighty times as harmful as carbon dioxide and it's leached out at every stage of production and transport. To enable its transport, import and export terminals have to be built, the impact of which some are estimating to be as harmful as coal in the coming years. With concerns over the future of LNG as a viable alternative, many are waiting to see what other options might come along rather than invest substantial sums in what might be only a stop-gap measure.

Methanol, cheap to produce and an emitter of less toxic emissions, was pursued as a possible replacement road transport fuel in the 1990s. However, being far less fuel-efficient than petrol meant far more would need to be used – and it's corrosive if left in place. Not ideal. Still, Maersk, the world's largest shipping company, said in 2021 that it's adding twelve container ships that would run on 'carbon-neutral' methanol (derived from biomass, or by combining hydrogen with carbon dioxide). It is just a handful of ships – but existing ships can also be retrofitted to run off methanol. While methanol produced from natural gas can cut emissions by up to 15 per cent, methanol from renewable sources can increase that 90 per cent. There's just one problem: finding sufficient supply of such 'green' methanol. To replace all marine fuel by 2050, green methanol production – from biomass or other sources – would have to top 500 million metric tonnes per year. That's over a hundred times current levels.

How about ammonia, more commonly used as a fertiliser? Various projects are looking at how it could be developed as a cleaner fuel for transport, in particular for shipping. But challenges abound. Ammonia is toxic and emits gases when burned. Plus traditional ammonia-manufacturing methods come with a considerable footprint, responsible for up to 2 per cent of global emissions. The answer to that would be the production of green ammonia, using a different method relying on renewable energy. But that's yet to be economically viable. When it is, it will also be a game changer for fertiliser production, shrinking farming's footprint (see Chapter 8).

What about biofuels, based on plant or animal waste or algae? After all, the technology to produce fuels such as hydrotreated vegetable oil or biomethanol is there. Again, though, they are relatively expensive to produce and not nearly as efficient an energy source as fossil fuels. With concerns too about finding sufficient sustainable source materials, scaling up would be a problem. Such fuels could be a valuable aid in weaning the industry off traditional fuel, but on their own do not produce a solution.

And so when it comes to the future of alternative energy sources, many governments, scientists and investors are taking inspiration from the very first element of the periodic table. Colourless, tasteless, highly combustible and the lightest element around, hydrogen has long been touted as a potential clean fuel source as during combustion it emits only water vapour. It makes up 90 per cent of the atoms in the universe and is most commonly found on Earth as water – H_2O – but it is rarely found in gas form, and so creating it is where the problem comes in.

Three main types of hydrogen fuel have been developed: grey, blue and green. Grey hydrogen is the one most used today. It is traditionally derived via a process of 'steam reforming', which is a way of splitting natural gas, but it uses fossil fuels to power the process.

Blue hydrogen is cleaner, but not perfect: the carbon emitted when producing the hydrogen is removed from the atmosphere using carbon capture and storage (CCS). This is where emissions from large-scale burning of hydrocarbons, in energy production or energy processes, are harnessed directly at the source and transported before being stored deep underground. Cleaning up the air in this fashion is touted as a key way of meeting climate targets. However, 10–20 per cent of emissions will still escape. And reducing emissions alone may not be enough.

The fossil fuel industry is keen on blue hydrogen, given that CCS is a way to keep using fossil fuels while mitigating their harms. For example, in its response to climate concerns, Exxon's focus is on emissions reduction rather than renewables, primarily using CCS. And the USA's 2022 Inflation Reduction Act proposed emissions limits for both new and existing power plants, based on the assumption of the availability of CCS technologies to funnel the carbon dioxide directly from plants before it reached the atmosphere, or using hydrogen as a fuel, on the back of investment into these areas. However, industry sources point out that such technologies simply can't function efficiently – yet – at scale. Several projects have overrun on budget and failed on targets.

That leaves us with the third type. Green hydrogen is carbon neutral. It relies on renewable generation, ideally derived from wind or solar, to power electrolysis to split water into its component parts. The technology exists to put hydrogen fuel cells on ships, which then generate heat and electrical energy to propel vessels. They are quiet and can be scaled up for larger ships. But hydrogen is less energy dense than bunker fuels – more gas would be needed, the cells would be bulkier, and as a result ships would have to carry less cargo – so it's less efficient for long voyages. The focus has been on trialling hydrogen-powered ferries doing shorter runs instead. Even so, renewable energy is still in short supply, as we've seen, so currently green hydrogen is expensive and cannot be produced in sufficient quantities to make an impact. Once it is viable, retrofitting ships and arranging for more frequent stops for refuelling will add to the costs of shipping lines.

Each kind of fuel currently has drawbacks. This is why ExxonMobil CEO Darren Woods has said, 'Today's alternatives to oil don't consistently offer the energy density, scale, transportability, availability – and most importantly – the affordability required to be widely accepted.'

It is also partly why industries such as shipping and aviation have been relatively slow to clean up their acts and have continued to belch out the filthiest fumes.

The focus of the shipping industry's environmental efforts thus far has largely been on reducing sulphur. Shipping fuel contains over 3,000 times as much of sulphur as diesel. Given that shipping has not been in the line of sight of most consumers, it took the International Maritime Organization (IMO), linked to the UN, over a decade to secure agreement among the diverse and scattered industry to limit sulphur content in fuels from 3.5 to 0.5 per cent, starting in 2020.

To achieve this, most shippers have opted to switch to cleaner, lower-sulphur fuel. The decision has huge economic ramifications. Resisting the shift was Saudi Arabia, a vast producer of traditional bottom-of-the-oil-barrel shipping fuel. In the other corner, producers of the less dense types of crude – the USA, for example – and major oil refiners such as BP were set to benefit.

And benefit they would: some analysts calculated that the moves could cost the shipping industry hundreds of billions, perhaps even $1 trillion dollars, just in the first few years of implementation as these fuels are more expensive. Such costs are usually passed on to retailers and, ultimately, consumers in the form of higher prices. However, shipping is a relatively small part of the cost of most items, and so for the majority of customers the increase will be a minor inconvenience rather than a crisis.

Sulphur is only one part of the problem. Ultimately the use of oil in any form leads to carbon emissions, so the shipping industry remains off course when it comes to meeting climate targets, largely due to the thorny issue of carbon, that 1 billion tonne elephant in the room, when measured in terms of the sector's emissions.

The industry is now acting quickly in response to fierce targets: industry bodies say it needs to halve its greenhouse gas emissions by 2050, compared to the 2008 figure. It's a tall order but just about doable – just 5 per cent of shipping fuel has to produce zero emissions by 2030 to put the industry on track to meet 2050 goals. Sourcing that amount of cleaner fuel should be possible, but environmentalists fear the plans are too timid.

More pressure is coming from regulators, too. The EU has proposed laws that would oblige shipping companies to pay for the carbon they emit travelling to or from ports in the bloc, and compel them to switch to lower carbon fuels. The International Chamber of Shipping is proposing a carbon levy of $2 per metric tonne to go towards the research and development of cleaner shipping fuels and technology.

The USA is going further than the IMO, and calling for the industry to reach net zero by 2050, with its Special Envoy John Kerry saying in 2023 that the technologies already exist; all that is lacking are the investment and will to scale up. As is often the case, this is a wholly different direction from the one charted by the previous US administration – another example of how politics can blow the journey to net zero off course.

In the boardroom, the biggest players know they need to start moving now. Maersk, for example, is aiming to reach net zero emissions by 2040. For meaningful change, the industry requires zero carbon fuels on a mainstream scale. Whichever fuel comes out on top will probably be more expensive, at least in the short term. The industry is increasingly braced for change that it knows will cost it billions more.

The same could be said for the aviation industry. Less than 10 per cent of goods by volume may reach our shores by air in the UK, but, by value, the proportion is far higher, as goods transported by air are often the most expensive. It's high-cost, low-density products, and those with a short shelf life that tend to make the grade: gemstones, precious metals and pharmaceuticals, for example.

The main demand for air travel comes from human cargo. A little over 2 per cent of carbon emissions come from air travel. It might not seem like a major issue, but on an individual basis, the problem is a far bigger deal. On average, fewer than one in twenty people around the globe fly regularly, so those emissions are being created by a very small percentage of the population.

When Covid-19 grounded planes, some queried if we'd reconsider our air-travel habits. Yet, with passenger numbers recovering by 2023, Airports Council International reckon passenger traffic worldwide could double to 19.3 billion in 2041. That sort of increase will outstrip expected gains on efficiency and emissions reduction.

Even though most people are aware of the impact of flying, they do not think it is enough to keep them out of the air. While various countries have levied taxes on air travel, some economists argue they are of little use as a deterrent. The most ardent flyers are those with deeper pockets or those for whom there is no viable alternative, both in terms of cost and convenience, to flying.

But while there's little pressure from passengers, carriers have been forced to take action following the scrutiny of policy-makers and investors. Carbon trading or offsetting programmes – where airlines effectively compensate for emissions by funding projects that restore degraded lands or replant trees – are now as familiar as the in-flight safety video. Yet campaigners claim such projects may fail to be effective on the ground.

Billions are also now being invested in cleaner aircraft and sustainable aviation fuels as part of a plan to halve 2005-level emissions by 2050. British Airways has signed up for sustainable aircraft fuel made from recycled cooking oils and other household waste, a deal that makes the scaling up of that process to an industrial and commercial level viable. It ran its first passenger flight partly powered by cooking oil in September 2021, from London to Glasgow. It aims to power a tenth of its planes using sustainable fuels by 2030.

In December 2021, United Airlines claimed it ran the first flight with one engine fully powered by sustainable fuels: a short hop between Chicago and Washington, with regular jet fuel in the other engine. Currently, the US air regulator has restrictions that allow only 50 per cent of fuels used in a jet plane to be sustainable because of concerns about performance. However, experts argue these regulations are increasingly outdated, that technology means alternative fuels are becoming ever more sophisticated.

Corn farmers have also joined up with airlines in the USA and successfully lobbied for tax credits to produce biofuels such as ethanol to power planes. Yet campaigners are unconvinced of the environmental benefits, saying the industry's calculations do not take account of the trees cut down to grow crops. And the price of ethanol could still be far higher than that of conventional jet fuel – up to three times as much. This is a cost that airlines, which are still trying to recover from the constraints of the pandemic, would not be able to bear without passing it on to customers.

Ultimately the raw materials simply do not exist in the quantities and forms needed for these fuels to be produced on a scale that could support major airlines in their entirety. (And if they did, those crops would require an awful lot of water.) What is currently being produced would account for just 0.1 per cent of the annual amount required.

Scaling that up would be expensive. United's CEO Scott Kirby says that converting just 10 per cent of the global aviation fuel supply to sustainable alternatives will require $250 billion in investment. He called for the US government to put up that stake. Plans from the Biden White House include tax credits for airlines that are worth $1.25 a gallon for fuels that reduce emissions by at least 50 per cent compared with jet fuel, and up to $1.75 per gallon for further reductions. With such incentives on the table, hopes are growing that alternative fuels could become a scalable and affordable alternative, but it won't happen overnight.

Given the limitations of alternative fuels, aircraft-makers themselves are taking on the challenge, with Europe's Airbus producing planes that can fly off green hydrogen. Once again, though, the similar problem exists in finding a sufficient and affordable source of that fuel.

The plans for the next generation of flying are being drawn up; in time they will become more viable. The question is whether that timescale will tally with the target that's been laid down for reducing the impact of air travel, towards which we're hurtling fast.

§

What else could be done to speed up the process? As well as climate targets and government pressure, the companies that use these transport services can make a difference to the way their goods are delivered around the world. The canniest retailers are getting ahead of the curve.

Multinationals such as Amazon, Ikea and Unilever are among those who have signed pledges to move goods only on ships with zero carbon fuel by 2040. Amazon founder Jeff Bezos has gone further, pledging to use his e-commerce giant's 'size and scale to make a difference'. Given that Amazon is worth more in sales than many mid-sized economies, its influence is considerable. The company has said it will be net zero by 2040. As part of that endeavour it has set up a $2 billion venture capital fund to back new technologies with an eye to decarbonising logistics. The projects funded range from short-range miniature electric aircraft used to deliver parcels, to a sustainable-fuel maker.

Measures such as these will help. Yet, as long as demand exists, oil producers will continue to meet it. However, given that some analysts predict that demand for oil will peak within the decade, the shrewdest producers are looking beyond 'peak oil' and making plans to power the transition. And that's when we'll start to see big changes.

One of the biggest oil-producing nations is Saudi Arabia. Before oil was struck in the 1930s, life in Saudi Arabia was largely a nomadic existence in a low-income subsistence economy. That was transformed when a US-owned well in Dhahran drilled into what would be the largest single source of petroleum in the world. Saudi is currently sitting on a sixth of the world's oil reserves. The superpowers this bestowed on the kingdom seemed to blossom into near-invincibility after a deal with the USA to price its oil in dollars. That cemented an interdepend-ence between the two nations, bestowing added protections and power on the world stage.

Oil might have given Saudi immense wealth and power, but it is also what's holding the country hostage in the desert. About 90 per cent of Saudi Arabia's exports consist of oil, providing half of its income. If patterns of consumption change – and it looks as though they will eventually – Saudi may be forced to find alternative sources of income. It's happening already. In summer 2023, for example, Saudi's sales of oil abroad dropped by a third, partly reflecting swings in price.

It may be some decades before the oil wells run dry but Saudi has long been stacking up the cash. Its powerful sovereign wealth fund has investments all over the world, the envy of many other oil-producing nations. But investments don't create jobs and a key plank of Saudi's vision is carving out prosperity for its people.

'A model of liveability putting people and planet in harmony for the twenty-first century and beyond . . . The future has a new home.' So boasts promotional materials for the new city state of Neom, the mega project from Saudi Arabia's contro-versial Crown Prince Mohammed bin Salman, its name derived from merging the Greek word for 'new' and the Arabic for 'future'. It promises homes for one million people, flying taxis, futuristic technology – and zero emissions.

It also nurtures Saudi Arabia's ambitions to carry on being the world's largest exporter of energy beyond the fossil fuel age as it contains a giant green hydrogen plant, built with the help of a US gas company and foreign money. Given that green hydrogen is ideally derived from wind or solar, what better place for a plant than the edge of the Saudi Arabian desert, where sunshine is pretty much guaranteed? Saudi Arabia wants to reap the rewards for keeping the lights on in the twenty-first century just as it kept the wheels turning in the twentieth. Although green hydrogen has become a holy grail in the energy transition, it's still a work in progress. The groundwork is being laid now, and the Saudis have the (considerable) funds to do it. But Saudi Arabia, along with its investors, is taking a gamble: whether the infrastructure can catch up quickly enough, and whether cheaper and more available alternatives might corner new markets. The benefits won't be felt for some years.

It's not just Saudi Arabia: from Canada to Australia via Iceland, many others are taking a gamble on green hydrogen now in the hope they too can be part of a new gold rush, and become major suppliers of a potential fuel of the future.

It feels a long way away but so too, not so long ago, did the click-and-deliver lifestyle. It might still be the case in a couple of decades that your internet purchase is powered by energy from the Middle East but this time from a far cleaner source and with a little less guilt attached.

5

The Daily Commute

Swapping petrol for electricity

Time to head to work, you slide into your brand-new car. Admittedly, it was a little on the pricey side, but you wanted an electric model. It's much better for the environment, and now that you don't have to keep filling up with expensive petrol, it will pay for itself eventually. Won't it?

A major move is afoot. As we've seen, the biggest contributor to carbon emissions is fossil fuels, and the main use of oil around the world is as road fuel. Keeping millions of vehicles on the road requires about 45 million barrels of the stuff every day. In pole position is the USA, which guzzles a fifth of that.

But the picture's changing fast as developing nations in particular play catch-up. In 2002, there were 800 million cars on the road; that is set to reach 2 billion by 2030. The issues that will create go way beyond gridlock.

For over a century, the fundamental design of the typical car has been unchanged. In functional terms, we're still looking at the internal combustion engine – as first launched for commercial production by Carl Benz in 1886 – linked to a mechanical transmission. Burn conventional fuel in that engine and, as well as carbon dioxide, you get a heady cocktail of emissions, including nitrous oxide, benzene and ozone, all of which contribute to global warming. It's also bad news for the lungs of the elderly, children and anyone whose respiratory system is at all compromised.

It didn't have to be this way. There was actually a little-known electric car design that pre-dates the standard petrol model. Anyos Jedlik, a Hungarian inventor, first fitted an electromagnetic device to a car in 1828. It wouldn't take him anywhere, being a small prototype model, but the first full-sized cars to use a rechargeable battery followed fifty years later. Quiet and easy to drive, they soon took off, making up a third of US sales in the early 1900s. Then their popularity shuddered to a halt. For this, we can blame Henry Ford, who introduced the world to the first affordable car in 1908. It wasn't just cheaper; it was easier to refuel too, thanks to the use of gasoline. And so petrol cars came to rule the road.

As we saw in Chapter 4, there will be no shortage of oil in the coming decades. But action is needed to prevent car emissions from spiralling. People still obviously need to get from A to B, so what we need are vehicles that aren't as polluting. It starts with car manufacturers.

§

Historically, car manufacturers have done their best to get around pollution legislation. The multi-trillion-dollar industry spends millions on lobbying to protect its interests, to influence policy-makers. For example, SUVs aren't only among the biggest and dirtiest beasts of the road, they're also the money-makers, providing hefty profit margins. They first came on the scene in the mid-1980s, combining rugged four-wheel-drive ability with the capacity of a minivan in an attempt to appeal to suburban Americans – even if their owners were doing little more than the school run or trips to the supermarket. Intense lobbying by the motor industry then meant that in the USA the new breed of vehicle was classed as a light truck, which, deemed as carrying out essential work, is subject to less stringent emission standards in America than your average traditional family car.

This desire for spacious vehicles – encouraged by car companies as a symbol of affluence – saw the bulky beasts doubling their market share between 2010 and 2018 globally, to account for almost two out of five car sales by the end of that period. It's increasingly a global trend, with SUVs accounting for one in two car sales in the USA and three in ten in India. If their drivers formed a nation in their own right, a study by the International Energy Agency (IEA) suggests they'd rank seventh globally for carbon emissions. In total, SUV use ranked second only to power generation in terms of contributing to the increase in carbon emissions between 2010 and 2018. They left heavy industry, trucks and even aviation in their wake. Even the analysts at the IEA were stunned by their findings. But car-makers across Europe and the USA have at times tried to resist legislative changes that would erode their profits.

Another example of car manufacturers trying to get around emissions is what has become known as the 'diesel dupe'. For years, diesel was pushed as a more environmentally friendly alternative to petrol, despite containing slightly more carbon. But diesel engines are termed 'low-burn'. As they combine less fuel with more air to get the same performance as a petrol engine, they emit 15 per cent less carbon dioxide into the air. So, as part of the EU's response to the 1997 Kyoto protocol commitment to lowering greenhouse gases, policy-makers threw their weight behind diesel vehicles, egged on by heavy lobbying from car-makers. Governments in Europe also encouraged their take up by ensuring diesel was cheaper than petrol. And it worked: in 1995, diesel cars accounted for less than 10 per cent of the UK market; by 2012 they made up more than half of sales.

Yet it turned out that diesel was not some cure-all. The vehicles in question emitted more toxic nitrogen oxides, known to exacerbate respiratory issues, than their petrol equivalents, as well as pumping out carcinogenic particulates, which are known to trigger asthma attacks and cardiovascular ailments. In 2012, the European Environment Agency found that nitrogen dioxide from diesel fumes contributed to 71,000 premature deaths across the continent in a single year.

Those findings pushed the car industry to make improvements. Filters to reduce the vast majority of particulate matter and technology were developed to reduce nitrous oxide emissions. The most efficient diesel vehicles were now on a par with their petrol cousins, claimed industry representatives.

So they said.

In 2015, the US Environmental Protection Agency served a notice of violation of the Clean Air Act to Germany's

Volkswagen. Independent tests, crucially performed on the road, had revealed that VW diesel cars were emitting toxic fumes at forty times the level the company claimed.

The cars, it transpired, had been fitted with a 'defeat device' – a computer program that allowed the car to detect if it was in (factory) test conditions, in which case it would switch to a less-polluting 'resting' phase. Put it out on the road, and the device was inactive and normal polluting business resumed.

There were 482,000 of these vehicles on US roads and 11 million affected worldwide, the result of massive promotion by VW, which had proclaimed the low emissions of its cars. Between them, they were invisibly chugging out up to 1 million tonnes more nitrous oxides than the company's claims had suggested.

Heads would roll and the company would pay out over £30 billion in compensation, fines and costs for sorting out the defective cars. Consumer trust had taken a colossal knock; the company's reputation lay in tatters. More widely, buyers simply didn't know if they were really choosing a vehicle with less environmental impact or not. Of course it was the environment – and people's lungs – that bore the irretrievable costs. There's no amount of money that can compensate for that. Nevertheless, it was an incident that helped trigger immense change in the wider car industry – changes that might otherwise have taken far longer.

Diesel was out of fashion, and not just for VW. It had become a dirty word across the globe, tainted by a scandal that had poisoned our air by stealth. Instead, the auto industry turned its attention to the rising popularity of electric cars. By 2023, diesel sales accounted for less than one in eight new cars registered in Europe, while battery-powered electric vehicles accounted for nearly one in five.

§

Sustainability and environmentally friendly messaging are de rigueur on a car-maker's website these days as governments and consumers increasingly look for ways to lessen the impact of our driving addiction.

One area that has been explored is alternative fuels. However, biofuels have a long way to go before they can replace oil (see Chapter 4), and it wouldn't be viable or economical to scale these up for mass use. Nor are those fuels without their environmental costs. There's also green hydrogen, but again the cost is a stumbling block, although it is one that could be diminished as investment from both public and private sources are poured into development. Japan and China are the leaders in vehicles powered by hydrogen cells.

And so it's electricity to which most people are turning. So far the biggest growth area has been in hybrid and electric vehicles. Those looking to buy a new set of wheels increasingly started turning to hybrid cars post-2015, a handy compromise for those who weren't ready to make the jump wholesale to purely battery-based cars but were concerned that the regulatory drive to phase out conventional models might leave their cars obsolete. Hybrids are powered by both an electric motor and a combustion engine, and the two can work together or separately. They're better for the environment than petrol cars in theory and cheaper than electric cars, as they contain a smaller battery, while also providing peace of mind that you're not entirely reliant on having a full charge. There are, admittedly, some doubts over their eco credentials, for example whether they burn more fuel than is claimed, and whether the emissions they save make up for those involved in producing their batteries, which, as we'll see, are not inconsiderable. Such models make up less than 10 per cent of the vehicle market but are projected to explode in popularity by 2030.

The same can be said for purely battery-powered electric cars. And as many countries have already set a date to ban the sale of hybrid cars – by 2035 in the UK and EU – it's these vehicles that have really become the focus for governments and car manufacturers.

Take General Motors, one of the world's biggest car-makers. In 2021, it snapped up an advertising slot during the USA's annual football Super Bowl, as you might have expected, but the ad itself was an emphatic shift in tone from a company that had initially supported the rollback of climate pollution rules under President Trump. It featured Hollywood star Will Ferrell, in typical tongue-in-cheek comedic mode, talking up GM's efforts to scale up electric vehicles, and comparing the USA's take-up of EVs to Norway's. It was a slick 60 seconds and the luxury models festooning the ad were a far cry from the frumpy but functional electric models that had previously made up GM's fleets. Their price tags were also far more likely to be within the reach of a normal American who might be dreaming of a Tesla.

The ad prompted some gentle ribbing from rival Ford on social media. Unlike GM, Ford retains a big presence in Europe and has been selling its battery electric Mach E in Norway. And it had opposed the rollback of emission standards under

President Trump. The exchange was a sign of how competitive the industry is and that batteries are the new battleground for car manufacturers. It also demonstrated how far the industry had travelled in a decade: in 2010 that super-prime Super Bowl ad slot featured Audi extolling the 'green' qualities of its A3TDI 'clean diesel' model.

According to the IEA, 10 million battery-powered electric vehicles (including hybrids) were sold in 2022, more than double the amount of just four years previously. Over half of the new models were in China. The IEA predicts that 240 million cars on roads will be electric or plug-in hybrids by 2030, more than 10 per cent of the total. In Europe and the USA they will make up the majority of sales, aided by regulation such as the USA's 2022 Inflation Reduction Act, which pledges subsidies for electric vehicle production, and tax breaks for those who buy them. That, the IEA suggests, means that demand for oil for road transport will peak in 2025.

It seems a simple road map for success. Replace a vehicle that burns fossil fuels and pumps its by-products into the air with one that runs off a battery that's recharged every so often. But of course it's not as straightforward as that. There are numerous issues that could potentially call an electric car's credentials into question, such as the environmental footprint of the car overall; the cost and availability of components; the impact of powering via electricity; the relative performance of the vehicles and batteries; and the availability of charging infrastructure.

A car's carbon footprint doesn't just fire up when it's driven off the forecourt. Any vehicle's journey follows a laborious trajectory: research and development, engineering, production, complex supply-chain logistics, distribution, after-sales service during use and eventually disposal. Manufacturing a car, for example, requires hundreds of components, such as aluminium, glass, leather, rubber and steel. All of those will be sourced from far-flung corners of the globe, each with their own supply chains and production implications. Such bulky items will also have to be shipped, creating their own footprint. As with textiles, keeping tabs on the environmental credentials of suppliers and source materials thousands of kilometres away is never easy. A car's usage might be the biggest contribution to its carbon footprint by far, but the other stages mean that while EVs can offer a significant reduction in emissions, they still have an environmental impact.

Some car-makers have already started addressing that, and have made advances in, for example, using recyclable raw materials such as hemp and recycled aluminium. Because of its sheer scale of operations, VW has even managed to scoop up and use metal trimmings that would otherwise have been wasted. Goals for recycling from regulators including the EU have helped focus minds but the automotive supply chain has a long way to go to achieve full circular sustainability. With 30,000 components in the typical car, ensuring every bit is reused, remanufactured and recycled – a truly circular model – is very challenging.

When it comes to the production line, there isn't much between the carbon footprint of a conventional vehicle's frame and its electric rival. The one big difference between them is to be found in the key ingredient: the battery. For the electric model, it will most probably be a lithium-ion battery, the most common type of rechargeable battery. This is a market already worth tens of billions, and according to McKinsey, forecast to hit $400 billion by 2030.

Heavy, as well as expensive, dangerous and carbon intensive to transport, these batteries are typically manufactured in proximity to the rest of the vehicle. That sounds as if it would be better for the environment. However, battery production itself can be heavy on emissions, particularly if located in Asia where the use of coal for electricity generation is more widespread (especially China, the source of more than seven out of ten batteries in 2023). Thanks to the mining and refining of raw materials and the manufacturing of the batteries, the production footprint of an electric vehicle vastly exceeds the production footprint of a typical internal-combustion-engine vehicle. Estimates vary but the manufacture of batteries can account for over 7 tonnes of greenhouse gas emissions, or over half the total involved in the production of those vehicles.

There are further complicating issues too, besides emissions. Manganese, cobalt, graphite and lithium are the core ingredients for electric batteries. They perform different functions but share a common trait: their reserves are highly concentrated in just a few places. China, Brazil and Turkey account for four-fifths of natural graphite, a crystalline form of carbon. Australia, Gabon, South Africa and Ukraine have a similar stranglehold on manganese. Chile has over a third of the world's lithium, while the DRC holds almost half of the cobalt.

That concentration poses some challenges when demand is soaring. It throws up issues of security of supply: conflict, political instability and environmental disasters can all jeopardise the availability of crucial raw materials. It also means that prices can be very volatile. What can be great news for producers might be less welcome for car manufacturers and their customers.

The gold rush for these raw materials can have social consequences too, one major example being the human rights issues surrounding the supply of cobalt (see page 56). Following the public outcry about this in 2019, European companies came together to create a new initiative to implement higher standards across the industry. BMW said it would source its cobalt for electric cars from Morocco and Australia and not the DRC.

Their US counterparts have been more reticent but have been investigating other options. Cobalt-free batteries, which rely on iron instead to create the positive charge, have been around for a while, but they've typically been less powerful and therefore offered less driving range. However, things are changing rapidly. In spring 2022, Tesla revealed that nearly half the vehicles it produced in the first quarter of 2022 were equipped with cobalt-free lithium iron phosphate batteries.

The one upside to these problems of supply is that they're propelling investment in green technology to lessen our dependency on these ingredients, and are making alternative sources more viable. For example, taking lithium from geothermal water found in places such as Germany and the USA is a far more carbon-friendly option than mining, which can contaminate water supplies, damage the soil and release carbon emissions.

The other issue is that these batteries have a shelf life; they last between ten and twenty years. Not bad, you might think; you'll have traded it in for a new model by then. But what then happens to the battery, which contains so many valuable resources? The cost and complexity of recycling lithium-ion batteries, to extract the various elements it contains, has traditionally been several times that of sourcing the raw material. As cobalt and nickel become more in demand, and thus more expensive, recycling is becoming a more viable way to source those elements. However, as iron is plentiful and far cheaper, recycling *those* batteries is less economical. A somewhat iron-ic development. If the future is electric, then there'll have to be greater emphasis on battery recycling. There might have to be government directives or company initiatives, perhaps due to consumer pressure propelling that investment.

Given the emissions involved in mining and battery production, electric cars have a carbon deficit relative to their conventional stablemates once they first hit the road. Can that be made up over a lifetime of use? Easily, is the answer.

Unlike vehicles with an internal combustion engine, electric ones have zero exhaust pipe greenhouse gas emissions. Some estimates suggest that on average they produce a twelfth of the carbon dioxide emissions per mile of a conventional petrol car. Typically, it takes only a year or two of driving for an electric vehicle to close the emissions gap with its traditional rival. The more you drive, the faster that deficit shrinks.

How the battery is fuelled does make a difference, however. Plug in that car to recharge the battery, and the electricity can come from any number of sources. While electricity generation is undergoing its own transformation, fossil fuels still play a part in many countries, to varying degrees. A Nissan Leaf electric vehicle driven in the UK would have, on average, a lifetime carbon footprint a third of that of a conventional vehicle. But the gap would be far narrower in Poland, say, which is more heavily reliant on coal to generate electricity. On average, the power source for EVs is already far cleaner than that of petrol vehicles but the overall benefit does depend on the speed and viability of a transformation towards cleaner electricity. As scrutiny and questions about energy security grow, progress is being made. In the UK, for example, the proportion of electricity generated from renewable clean sources grew from a fifth to almost a half in the space of a decade.

The precise lifetime carbon costs of each vehicle will depend on a multitude of factors: model, size, driving patterns and weather conditions for a start. Smaller newer cars tend to produce less emissions. A speed of about 55 mph is typically the most energy efficient, as long as it's steady – studies have found that frequent deceleration and acceleration can be hugely detrimental when it comes to emissions and particulates. Regardless of these factors, however, EVs have the upper hand.

While the environmental costs are lower with an EV, consumers might still wonder about their financial costs. The running costs of an electric vehicle are far lower than those of a car with an internal combustion engine. In addition to no longer needing to fill the tank, the maintenance needs are lower and so less financially punishing. They may still need servicing, but the engines of electric cars contain far fewer moving parts, as do the gearboxes. In short, there's less capacity for them going wrong and needing repair. Prior to 2022, by charging an electric car at home, the running cost of such a vehicle was less than half that of its conventional cousins. After Russia's invasion of Ukraine, the price of electricity soared, almost eradicating the cost advantage by late 2023. That surge in price is subsiding but it goes to show that even if you choose electric, you can still fall prey to the whims of fossil fuel markets.

Of course, the upfront cost of an electric car remains far higher, and that is what puts some people off. Internal combustion engine cars have been produced commercially for a century, and as the electric newcomers aren't yet produced at the same mass scale they haven't been able to compete on price. But as the appetite grows, and governments continue to subsidise production, manufacturers and their customers will be able to benefit from economies of scale. To help incentivise consumers to buy electric or hybrid vehicles – and sometimes to scrap older gas belchers – governments have stepped in to offer tax breaks. That's not just on purchase, but also on motor tax once it hits the road. However, governments have to approach any additional taxation with caution, particularly when it widens the running costs between petrol and electric vehicles.

Taxes on petrol are regressive. The lower your income, the larger the proportion paid in such duties; it's a levy that falls hardest on the masses. While eco-friendly governments see tax incentives as a way of nudging drivers away from fossil fuels and their road-clogging hosts, they're also perceived by some as curbing the right to a particular lifestyle. London's Ultra Low Emissions Zone (ULEZ) scheme, under which drivers whose vehicles do not meet emissions standards pay more to drive in the capital, has been criticised in some quarters for hitting poorer and more vulnerable people disproportionately, while the scheme's impact on emissions has been debatable. In France, the *gilet jaune* protests (named after the yellow vests worn by demonstrators) began as a grassroots organisation, instigated by rising fuel prices. The movement brought parts of the country to a standstill for over two years. As of 2023, successive UK governments have overridden existing legislation and kept fuel duty frozen for over a decade; effectively drivers have hung on to £50 billion more than they otherwise would have. Politicians know that such taxes are a particularly sensitive area for the electorate – but environmentalists argue that a freeze just helps to give petrol a green light.

This also highlights another car problem for governments: fuel taxes mean that spinning wheels are big money-spinners for them. If they offer too many tax incentives, there will come a tipping point where electric cars are so popular that the incentive schemes become unaffordable – and somewhat redundant. At that point, governments might have to find alternatives, perhaps looking at road pricing, the sort of tolls on motorways that are commonplace in parts of Europe.

Consumers also suffer from range anxiety – the fear that electric cars simply won't be able to get you to where you want to go, leaving you stranded. Medicating this requires two remedies: improving the batteries and the adequate provision of charging infrastructure. Both are changing rapidly. For example, the first Nissan Leaf claimed a battery range of 160 kilometres in 2011. Its successor, unveiled just a few years later in 2017, has a claimed range of 380 kilometres. Many other models have surpassed that. And by the end of 2022, globally there were 2.7 million public charging points – almost a million more than just a year previously, with service stations installing more banks of chargers. Growth in China has been particularly marked, especially in densely populated cities. It now has 1.8 million public charging points and in 2022 sold four electric vehicles for every one sold in the US in 2022. By contrast, growth has been much slower in America, where suburban homes are much more likely to have space for a private point. To further reassure drivers, there is an increasing array of apps to help plot journeys and charging breaks.

What about having sufficient power for electric cars? Is there enough electricity to support mass electric car ownership, and do the wires that carry electricity have adequate capacity? The UK's National Grid points out that energy efficiency gains over the last couple of decades mean that the country is using less electricity. It claims that even if every household had an electric vehicle, electricity use would not reach the levels of twenty years ago. Regulations have been introduced to ensure that charge points will allow the charging to happen when there is less demand on the grid, or when more renewable electricity is available via smart functionality. It's a similar picture in the USA.

So on balance, while there are still improvements to be made, it seems that EVs are indeed better for both the environment and consumers' wallets, once you've stomached the initial outlay.

§

The clear benefits of EVs mean they are on the rise, but they're still in the minority. Making the switch entirely will take some time, as the big picture is more complicated than it might appear as competing interests come into play. It's not easy to force through large-scale change quickly. India is an interesting case to consider. It is one of the countries driving the global increase in road vehicles, but it has plans to make them as green as possible.

The Indian government's target is for 30 per cent of private vehicle sales to be electric by 2030. In 2017, Nitin Gadkari, India's minister of road transport and highways, left his audience of auto-makers speechless when he announced the move towards alternative fuels in no uncertain terms: 'I am going to do this whether you like it or not,' Gadkari said. 'And I'm not going to ask you. I'm going to bulldoze it.'

The target is not as ambitious as in other major countries – the UK's aim is to phase out sales of new petrol and diesel cars by 2035 – but India faces more roadblocks to get there.

One of the reasons the government is determined to take action is that India hosts twenty out of the thirty most polluted cities on the planet. And the country is a rarity among big economies in that its fossil fuel emissions are still on the rise. Much of that is down to industrial activity, but vehicles are making a growing contribution. India's road to riches has meant the rise of urbanisation – an exodus from villages to cities, from field to factory and data centres. Currently fewer than 50 out of every 1,000 Indians owns a car – contrast that with around 400 in the UK and over 850 per 1,000 in the USA – but that rate is rising. Already, the sheer number of people in the most populous country on Earth is enough to put it in the top three in terms of the absolute number of passenger cars populating the roads (outranked only by the USA and China). That number is set to balloon, with car ownership predicted to double every eight to ten years. Achieving its 2030 target could save India about £15 billion a year in oil imports.

However, the government has to balance other economic interests. India, long a laggard on the manufacturing scene, also wants to fill in its manufacturing gaps, and car production is virtually revered in many nations as a source of skilled (and thus well-paid) manufacturing jobs and a massive source of trade in goods. The finance minister has expressed the wish for Indian auto-makers to leapfrog their rivals, with an initiative going by the acronym FAME (Faster Adoption and Manufacturing of Hybrid and Electric Vehicles). But the prosaic reality is that it might take some time. There is some progress here: India has attracted interest as a centre of frugal engineering, offering up budget versions of products with enough added value and nods to local preferences to appeal to a rapidly expanding middle class. Hence the arrival of a $5,000 passenger car that drew heavily on a local supply chains. But it's a far cry from mainstream electric vehicles. Those can cost at least twice as much, often far more. Although the biggest players are offering electric vehicles, there remains a lack of affordable options in the sector that makes up over two-thirds of the Indian car market: compact models that can last for a long distance without needing a top-up.

That's why there was an almighty pushback from the Indian car industry to the government's ambitions, which claimed that millions of jobs across the supply chain could be at risk. Within two years the focus shifted to two-wheelers and three-wheelers (auto rickshaws). Fewer spokes maybe, but not to be sniffed at: their sales outnumber those of passenger cars by over six to one in India.

Electrification is still high on the agenda though. India's government has offered capital grants for organisations promoting the use of EVs, and launched two Expressions of Interest for organisations who want to offer charging stations. The government wants to see charging stations at all 69,000 petrol stations, but that's just a fraction of what's needed if EV ownership is going to reach the heights the government dreams of. And it's still a long way off. In January 2023, India had fewer than 5,000 public charging stations – not even one charging station per hundred EVs. The average globally is more like one to ten. Improving that will be key to the country's EV ambitions.

The contracts the Indian government awarded to bidders after the first Expression of Interest went to public organisations. But the industry is taking matters into its own hands. Tata Motors has said it will offer charging points in its retail outlets, in addition to the points its sister company, Tata Power, is offering around the country. It's part of a holistic approach the group is taking, widening its range of offerings and also developing lithium-ion batteries and battery packs within its stable. It's part of a bid to re-establish the dominance of the car-maker, which has been kept away from pole position by rivals Maruti and Hyundai.

If all goes to plan, electric mobility is India's domestic road-bound gold rush, but there's a lot of work and vision involved. It helps that some essential raw materials are found there. Research institutes and universities can investigate alternatives to expensive and in-demand lithium-ion batteries (such as those based on carbon) and other technologies that would help boost the availability of lower-cost mass-scale production capabilities (and reduce reliance on China, the region's leader in battery manufacture). Ultimately, a lot will depend on coordination, not just along the production and consumption line, but also across government and civil society. Companies will have to bring investment and technical know-how if they're to meet the challenge.

To realise its electric dream, the Indian government has further to go in creating an ecosystem that nurtures a revolution among car-makers and consumers. With 80 per cent of passenger traffic going via heavily congested roads, the state is leading the charge on an ambitious road-building boom, but from construction to engineering, private companies are also stepping up their game. The Indian government has earmarked over a trillion dollars to upgrade the nation's travel networks. Ironically, it's heavy industry – from steel to car-making – that would be the biggest beneficiary of turbo-charging mobility infrastructure. The electric revolution is happening, and it's speeding up. But every country faces its own challenges – economic barriers, technological advances, consumer attitudes or political will – in making it a reality as quickly as possible.

~

Despite all of this, it remains true that no matter how beneficial electric cars might be, the most environmentally friendly car is . . . no car at all.

Trains, buses, coaches, trams . . . public transport generally has a far lower carbon footprint than its more exclusive cousin. But it has to be convenient, affordable, comprehensive – and appealing. To tick the green box, it also ideally needs to be going electric. Oslo, a city that once flourished on the proceeds of fossil fuel reserves, is now aiming to be the world's first emissions-free city by 2030. As part of that it is trying to become the first capital city with an all-electric public transport system, replacing its diesel buses with 450 electric ones. The move would also save the city millions of euros in fuel. But it hit a snag when a particularly cold winter took some out of service, after the extreme chill impacted both the batteries and the range of the buses. One solution mooted by academics was installing diesel heaters to relieve the strain on the batteries on particularly cold days. It's not always plain sailing.

Other urban centres are looking into green alternatives: coffee waste, old cooking oil and animal tallow are among the unusual sources of fuel for some London buses. Dozens of other European cities have encouraged their drivers to ditch the car by making public transport free. Luxembourg became the first country to scrap public transport charges nationwide in 2020; Malta followed shortly after.

The degree and reach of public transportation varies the world over, but it's generally seen as a force for good – and not just in environmental terms. Every £1, ₹1, €1 or $1 spent on a railway or road delivers overall economic gains far in excess of that initial outlay, moving workers or goods around faster and more efficiently. It is often profitable, too; in many countries, the funding of public transport is generally evenly split between private and public sector.

Nevertheless, even a world-class speedy, safe and comfortable transport network may not get you from A to B. Public transport focuses on connecting centres to centres. What keeps urban planners – and those determined to keep us out of cars – awake is the last-mile problem. How do you get travellers from a public transport hub to their final destination? Forget the last mile, anything over a quarter of that distance has commuters thinking twice about the viability of public transport. Small wonder that, even in the relatively well-connected UK, four out of five journeys that exceed a mile happen in a car.

With rickshaws among the top of the government's go-electric priority list, India already has one answer to the last-mile conundrum. Another is bicycles – a long-used solution born out of affordability and need rather than concerns about environmental consequences. And of course there's the cheapest mode of transport of all: walking.

Perhaps surprisingly, the transition to pedal and foot power is more of a challenge the more affluent the country. While Germany, Denmark and the Netherlands have policies dating back to the 1970s and 1980s that make cycling a cultural norm, that is far less true of countries such as the USA and UK. Environmental concerns mean the tide is slowly turning there too, with tax incentives for workers to buy bikes in the UK, and free cycling lessons on offer. There were 300 such incentive schemes in force in Europe by 2023.

What has revolutionised two-wheel travel in many city centres is the advent of cycle sharing and hiring schemes, a novelty at the turn of the millennium, now a feature in 1,500 cities around the globe. Some originated as not-for-profit or community projects, some – as in Paris or London – are private–public partnerships. The growth of cycle highways and superhighways has also made it safer for cyclists to venture out. In 2022, one in five UK adults said they used a bike once a week, while in the USA it was actually higher at one in four. In India, the federal government is jumping on the pedals too with bike-sharing schemes and car-free Sundays piloted in some cities.

A number of enterprising private companies have set up around the globe, in particular offering dockless bikes, but it hasn't always been a smooth ride. China's Wukong bike failed to survive the journey after making the fundamental error of failing to include GPS, making tracking and location services tricky, and theft an inevitability. Its much larger stablemate Bluegogo went flat after simply struggling to make it in an overcrowded market.

Car club schemes have had more success. Zipcar saw membership in London more than double between in 2018 and 2020. Cities have proved to be the most popular for such schemes due to the costs of parking vehicles, ease of collection and the fact that most journeys are quite short.

What all these operators have in common is that they're part of the so-called sharing economy, a very twenty-first-century phenomenon. It works by capitalising on underused assets, saving time and space and money. It also ticks all the boxes for urban hipsters, who want to flash those green credentials. But, as you don't actually get a share of that asset, the 'sharing' label could be construed as clever marketing by the originators in Silicon Valley. Economists argue it's better referred to as 'the access economy'. Fancy terms apart, it's simply another rental service, just in the digital age.

Like any other business, private companies pulling the strings of the sharing economy are doing it for the cash rather than for love. In some ways, the rules for making money out of the access economy are no different from any other enterprise: find a product that there's excess desire for and provide it. Ideally, too, if you're in this business you want a supportive infrastructure. If you're renting out bikes, you want pedal-friendly routes such as cycle highways and well-lit paths. Hills are your enemy, as are laws making the wearing of helmets mandatory.

In fact, laws, full stop, tend to be enemy of the access economy operators – or, as they prefer to be known, the disruptors. Now ubiquitous in cities, the likes of Uber and Lyft refer to themselves as ride-hailing apps, revolutionising affordable taxi rides for users and providing self-employment opportunities to their drivers. To their detractors, including some trade unions and existing taxi operators, they're aggressive cab companies that attempt to corner the market and push out the incumbents through cut-price competition, underpinned by cutting corners in areas such as safety and workers' rights. Cheap and ethical can be tricky to find in the same sentence.

Overall, while in environmental terms the best car would be no car at all, that solution is simply unrealistic for most people. Those living in more urban areas might be able to rely more on public transport, taxis, bikes or even walking, but once you get into the countryside, the distances involved and less localised demand make functioning without personal transport a trickier prospect. A vast revolution in public transport might be needed, not just in the way it is fuelled but also its range and scope, in order to the reduce the relative attractiveness of car ownership. But given the problem of the 'last mile', and ingrained attitudes, private car ownership is here to stay.

§

Like so many 'green' changes, the push to electric vehicles – or no vehicles at all – requires immense investment in infrastructure. Governments are trying to help companies and consumers to phase out oil as smoothly as possible, without having an adverse effect on their economies.

Seismic change on this scale requires high levels of coordination and buy-in, something policy-makers the world over have sometimes failed to take on board. To instigate an automotive revolution, governments need to take all stakeholders with them: vendors, car-makers, spare part manufacturers, mechanics, providers of charging stations – and consumers. Making bullish announcements such as that of India's transport minister in 2017 is the motoring equivalent of putting the cart in front of the horse. Creating a greener way of travel needs a joined-up approach across political, economic, legal, industrial and social structures. A government issuing directives, even with consumers amenable to change, is not enough. The automobile first built by Carl Benz is here to stay; the focus needs to be on making it more fit for the twenty-first-century planet – and its people. Car-makers have shown themselves capable of sweeping change, but it's the consumers – and their tastes and attitudes – who are in the driving seat.

6

Buying a Coffee

Overhauling plastics and the disposable lifestyle

As the afternoon draws on, you need a pick-me-up. Maybe a fresh burst of inspiration – and caffeine – from the coffee shop around the corner. Although, you realise with a pang of guilt, you forgot your reusable cup; it'll have to be a disposable plastic one. And now you think about it, you did that yesterday – and last week. Old habits are so hard to break, and the disposable consumer lifestyle is just so convenient . . . But it is, of course, littered with plastics and packaging.

That disposable lifestyle has been the status symbol of rising disposable incomes. Single-use plastics are effective and convenient as a vessel for so many different products, from a cup of coffee to a bottle of soda. As we'll see, it's a habit harder to break than caffeine, and the most hardened addicts are particularly resistant to change.

The type of plastic that's most commonly used for cups and bottles – polyethylene terephthalate, or PET – is formed from naphtha, a substance refined from crude oil. Naphtha is then subject to a complex process known as polymerisation, which involves high heat, pressure and a catalyst, to produce pellets that can be moulded into containers. For all that, plastic packaging isn't the biggest enemy when it comes to combating climate change. It accounts for a tiny proportion of fossil fuel usage, perhaps as little as 3 per cent. So, are our habits such a big deal? Well, there's another problem with plastic, one that's become emblematic of the challenge consumers have to grasp: global plastic waste totalling 353 million tonnes in 2019.

Broadcast in over thirty countries – including the USA and China – the finale of BBC's *Blue Planet II* in 2017 prompted outrage and alarm for millions when presenter Sir David Attenborough highlighted the tragedy plastics are visiting on the world's oceans. From baby dolphins poisoned by microscopic shards of plastic to tiny albatrosses injured by disposable toothpicks, it laid bare the human-made threat to marine life. Deep-sea currents mean that the greatest patches of plastic pollution can lie in the most remote areas. One has been dubbed the Great Pacific Garbage Patch and supposedly covers an area of 1.6 million square kilometres. While recording the terrible consequences of our actions, one camera operator had to free a sperm whale that had become entangled in a discarded plastic bucket, while one of his colleagues rescued a hawksbill turtle that was caught up in a plastic bag.

In total, there are an estimated 5 trillion pieces of discarded plastic in the ocean, over 600 for each person on the planet. The most comprehensive study of ocean waste so far, carried out by Spanish academics at the University of Cádiz, found that single-use bags, plastic bottles, food containers and food wrappers together make up almost half of the human-made waste in those waterways. It would appear that snacks and sugary drinks aren't a no-no just for their calorific content.

All this rubbish is far more than an offshore eyesore. The UN reckons 90 per cent of seabirds will have ingested it, and bigger objects can prove fatal. Plastic also eventually breaks up into microplastics – the technical term for pieces less than 5 millimetres in length. Over a quarter of fish are assumed to have consumed microplastics and, as fish enter the food chain, they've also inevitably become part of the human diet. Being so new to the game, scientists are still unsure of the exact impact they have on animal or human health. Consultant Deloitte estimates that the annual global cost of marine plastic pollution ranges between $6 and $19 billion, when factoring in the impact on tourism, fisheries and aquaculture, and the cost of state funded clean-ups.

Non-profit organisation Ocean Cleanup has taken up the challenge of removing 90 per cent of floating plastic from the oceans by 2040, clearing up what's already there and preventing it leaching into waterways in the first place. Its partners include Coca-Cola and shipping giant Maersk, brands that often crop up in debates over plastic pollution. It's been trialling, at a cost of £20 million, a giant 600-metre artificial U-shaped barrier that effectively corners and scoops up plastic. By 2022, the organisation was boasting of the ability to collect 10,000 kilograms of waste in the space of five days. But, like many new technologies, it hasn't been without its hurdles. Early attempts saw plastic captured but then managing to escape. Some scientists are querying the overall effectiveness of the system, concerned that the process itself could be polluting and risk harming sea life, and might not be successful at scooping up those microplastics. Ultimately its usefulness will be limited if we simply carry on chucking more in.

Plastic doesn't just threaten marine life; larger items pose a threat to land animals that ingest them as well, while microplastics also degrade soil quality, impacting the nutrient uptake of plants. And when plastic is simply sent to landfill, it releases the greenhouse gas methane as it degrades.

Without drastic action, the OECD estimates the amount of global plastic waste could almost triple by 2060. It's increasingly hard to hide from the mess we've created. Yet we seem reluctant to change our ways, particularly when the alternatives mean compromise on price or convenience.

§

It is countries in the developing world such as Malaysia and the Philippines that rank among the top contributors to plastic waste in the ocean. In part, that's because those nations are adopting the West's disposable lifestyle and have long coastlines in relation to their landmass. But America too has been literally exporting its plastic problem.

The USA accounts for 4 per cent of the world's population but about 12 per cent of its waste: the average citizen typically chucks out twice their body weight in plastic every year, making the USA a greater polluter of such material than all the countries in the European Union put together. The nation's awash in a sea of single-use plastics, their use, for the most part, attached to far less social stigma than in Europe.

The average American consumes double their body weight in sugar every year and half of that comes from soda and other sugary drinks. The campaign group Break Free From Plastic conducts an annual audit of refuse from over fifty countries, monitoring discarded branded packaging in parks, beaches and other public spaces. Its 2022 results showed Coca-Cola leads the way as the top source of plastic polluters, with 85,000 branded plastic pieces. Bitter rival PepsiCo followed with 51,000 and sweet-maker Nestlé had third place with 27,000.

It's perhaps an inevitable side effect for Coke, given that it's the most popular soft drink in almost every country (Scotland with its fluorescent Irn-Bru is among the notable exceptions). And in terms of consumption per head, the USA is second only to Mexico.

Coca-Cola has come a long way from its origins. The drink was the concoction of pharmacist John S. Pemberton, who designed the beverage in 1886 as a tonic to ease the pain of ailments he suffered when he was a colonel in the Confederate Army in the American Civil War. Long gone are the days when it contained alcohol and cocaine. Still lingering, however, is the iconic bottle. The 'contour' design was intended to make the drink stand out – and it did, making the cover of *Time* magazine in the 1950s. But while the shape remains, its substance has changed, with the original glass giving way to plastic.

Engineer Nathaniel Wyeth patented PET bottles in 1973. They were a game changer in the fizzy-drinks industry: portable, cheap and, unlike other plastic predecessors, able to withstand the pressure of carbonated liquids. The bottles were not just unbreakable and light but resealable: just screw the lid back on and preserve the bubbles.

Almost half a century on, 70 per cent of the world's soft drinks – from water to sodas – are packaged in such bottles. Coca-Cola alone churns out the equivalent of 200,000 PET plastic bottles every minute; small wonder they'll pop up more often than their competitors. But the bottles have been relegated from marvel to liability.

Many people are looking to corporations such as Coca-Cola to help curb plastic pollution. Plastic can be recycled two or three times before the material starts to degrade, so one way to reduce the volume of plastic in the environment is to recycle the bottles we already have. Like its rivals, Coca-Cola has targets to reduce the use of virgin plastics, aiming for all packaging to contain 50 per cent recycled material by 2030. It has a way to go: by 2022 it had got to 25 per cent for all packaging, and only about 15 per cent when it came to PET plastic. As it points out, the use of material for food-grade products has to be of higher standard and requires the support of policy and technology. But all the mega purveyors of snacks and fizzy drinks also face another problem: cost.

Attempts to introduce more recycled content into plastic bottles actually stretches back a few decades, but the price of recycled material made it uneconomic even to the biggest names in the business in those early days.

As technology evolved, that cost came down drastically. But then emerged another hurdle. The thirst for recycled plastic has been growing stronger, to the point of becoming insatiable. And supply simply can't keep up. It's partly because not enough plastic is being recycled around the world, so there aren't enough raw materials available.

In the USA, fewer than a third of PET drinks bottles were recycled in 2019. That, according to a report from the Recycling

Partnership, means that there's a shortfall of about 450 million kilograms between what's collected and what soft-drink-makers will need if they are to meet their 2025 targets for recycled content. To get there, the recycling rate would have to get to one in two. In 2020, California became the first US state to mandate for recycled content in the bottles of drinks sold there: 15 per cent by 2022, 25 per cent in 2025 and 50 per cent in 2030. The biggest players – Coca-Cola, Nestlé and PepsiCo, for example – were able to comply with the first edict. But over 500 smaller manufacturers did not. And that may not be for want of trying but because of a struggle to compete for the materials themselves. Targets and laws are hamstrung if there aren't the raw materials needed for recycled PET (rPET to its friends).

What's more, plastic can't be infinitely recycled. A study by consultants Eunomia claimed new bottles on the EU market contained an average of just 17 per cent recycled material, which it said was instead often 'downcycled' into lower-quality products such as plastic trays, strapping or fibres.

The supply problem starts at the doorstep, where in the USA a myriad of rules, kerbside collection facilities, suitable bins and even ignorance can choke off the desire to recycle. Those plastics that are collected may be discarded if they are contaminated by food waste. Where initiatives do exist, they tend to rely on local city or state funds, which can be easily withdrawn in times of fiscal need or according to political whim. It's a far cry from some areas in Europe where citizens live in fear of fines for putting out the wrong sort of trash.

What some states have done is borrow a trick from nostalgia: offer a refundable deposit of 5 or 10 cents on PET bottles.

The scheme also provides a potential boost for taxpayer funds but it's yet to catch on at a national level.

A more comprehensive policy on collecting, sorting and cleaning plastic is needed. Campaigners say that'll take more than the government is putting on the table, and will need households to be compelled to take part. For the policy to be truly effective, they say that a form of the Extended Producer Responsibility legislation being rolled out in the UK (which dictates that a business must shoulder the cost of the waste created by its products throughout their entire life cycle) should apply to American businesses too. However, US politicians may see this as an infringement too far.

It is possible to recycle more, as other countries have demonstrated. The UK has seen its recycling rates of plastic bottles shoot up from 3 per cent to 60 per cent in the last couple of decades. In Japan, a combination of stringent laws and compliant consumers has resulted in a figure closer to 90 per cent. Across the EU, where ten countries started operating a deposit scheme as of 2022, the recycling rate is almost 50 per cent.

But to what end? Where do these bottles go when they leave your local bin? Some of the recycling happens thousands of kilometres away from where the plastic was used. Hundreds of thousands of tonnes of plastic are shipped from the USA to developing nations every year, often to countries that are poorly regulated or are struggling to process their own refuse. Some don't possess the necessary – or even any – formal recycling processes for the waste but are willing to take it for the payment, while those offloading it can add the consignment to their recycling claims. Import bans imposed by Turkey and China, says the World Economic Forum, led to over 100 million kilograms less US-originated plastic being recycled over the course of a year, a drop of around 5 per cent. Turkey's ban, however, was reversed within the year.

Outsourcing the plastic waste heap is a habit of some of the more ardent recyclers too. The UK sends around 1.5 million tonnes of packaging waste abroad every year, with Turkey the most popular destination. However, the waste is not always recycled, often being either dumped or burned, which releases toxic chemicals into the air, food chain and water sources. Turkey's recycling rate around is 12 per cent, below that of any other higher-income country. Following reports of waste being dumped or burned in Turkey with 'irreversible and shocking' environmental and health implications, in 2022 British law-makers called for the practice of exporting waste to be ultimately banned and for it to be processed at home instead. But that was rejected by the government, which claimed legitimate exports have a role in the management of UK waste.

Poor waste management and a lack of oversight are factors, but some of the plastic dumped or burned isn't suitable for recycling. Many crisp packets are laminates, that is plastic mixed with other materials. If something isn't pure plastic, it can't be recycled. Nor can the plastic be repurposed if it is contaminated by foodstuffs. Laminates or anything tainted with food or dirt is destined for landfill or waterways. That's partly why recycling, say campaigners, is no magic bullet.

To tackle the issue, 187 countries have signed a pact restricting the import of plastic waste, to protect against the dumping of contaminated or otherwise unsuitable plastics. For rich countries looking to boast of cutting down on plastic waste, that quick and dirty route remains a tempting one. However, progress is being made in some areas: it is possible to capture methane at landfill sites, with the right investment, and recycling facilities are improving.

The USA's ability to reprocess the amount collected on home soil is increasing. That amount had doubled over a decade to over 725 million kilograms in 2020, in part due to the laws passed in China in 2018 banning the import of scrap plastic. Its increasing ability to be a larger player in the rPET industry will benefit the country as beverage-makers and others jostle for material to meet targets.

As things stand, the scarcity of recycling meant that by late 2019, the cost of the recycled flakes used for bottles and other packaging had overtaken that of virgin plastic, and that margin widened further in the early 2020s. Ethical practice was in danger of becoming a luxury product for the drinks producers with the deepest pockets – or the most diligent shareholders or affluent customers. One study said it could cost European drinks-makers $250 million per year, at that point, to stick with their recycled components. One European drinks industry body referred to rPET as 'becoming almost as rare as white truffles or gold' as it highlighted that it's the smaller manufacturers that are struggling to get rPET, even when it's derived from their own products, as the material is procured through a bidding process and so preference is given to the giants with the deepest pockets.

The gulf between recycled and virgin PET costs was also exacerbated by a surge in shale-gas production in the USA that started in 2005, which drove down the cost of the petrochemicals used in PET. In particular, ethylene is a vital component of polymers, including PET, and a fifth of the global supply comes from the USA's Gulf Coast, where petrochemical hubs thrive on a plentiful gas supply.

So, despite the rising popularity of recycled PET, the USA is looking to boost its plastic production. The country is not just the biggest devourer of plastic packaging; it's feeding its own appetite. It also churns out polypropylene for carpets and furniture, and PVC plastics for toys. The industry poses a challenge in the fight against climate change, but it also supports a million jobs, so is not one the USA is going to just wind down.

With demand set to soar even faster in Asia, US companies are eyeing a greater foothold in this industry, just as many users of plastic packaging in Europe have their wings clipped by stricter environmental legislation. After all, the USA, the home of the once booming but now buckled Rust Belt, wants to retain and boost the industries where it retains a competitive advantage. With other countries increasingly aspiring to the disposable lifestyle they've espied in Hollywood movies, and to which plastics are so central, it is entirely rational to want to profit from that.

The plastics industry, however, has taken a few knocks in the past few years. The frequency of hurricanes hitting the Gulf Coast is on the rise. The death and devastation wrought by Hurricane Katrina left painful scars etched deep in the area. But it is far from the only one. In September 2022 Hurricane Ian battered the region once again, leaving 2 million people and businesses without power. The fortunes of the area responsible for over four-fifths of America's plastic production are often at the mercy of increasingly frequent weather 'events'.

In such challenging times, supporting the plastics industry requires a delicate balancing act. In the 2022 Inflation Reduction Act, President Biden's approach to curbing the plastic explosion centred on a mere $14.5 million earmarked to improve the recycling technologies for used plastics and developing new recyclable plastics. Critics said it was too watered down, stymied by Republican opposition to the point that it had become more about supporting industry than installing meaningful change; cleaning up the after-effects of the USA's plastic diet rather than reducing its intake. It's such a tiny amount relative to a $400 billion industry, it's effectively business as usual. The USA clearly wants to retain its plastic cake and eat it.

Meanwhile, measures to impose outright targets or curbs on single-use plastic are still on the legislative drawing board, and face fierce opposition. Those million American livelihoods relying on plastics manufacturing are a considerable hurdle, as is changing the American mindset. But President Biden's strategy was still a departure from his predecessor's. It is not to be scoffed at, for the USA lags woefully behind in many aspects of the circular economy.

∽

But does the future have to be plastic? If we're struggling to recycle, and to cut down on our usage, we need alternatives. While 70 per cent of the world's soft drinks are encased in it, the other 30 per cent relies on glass, aluminium or treated paper. Should that be the wholesale way forward?

In 2020 at the World Economic Forum in Davos, eyebrows were raised when Coca-Cola's head of sustainability said that single-use plastic would remain at the heart of its product line. Bea Perez claimed that customers still wanted the lightweight packaging, and so ditching plastic outright would alienate customers and damage sales. What the customer wants, the customer gets – that is, if you want to make a profit and stay in business for another 150 years.

Are customers so resistant to the idea? A survey conducted shortly after by Piplsay showed 51 per cent of Americans would buy Coke even if the bottles were heavier or came in non-sealable packaging. But that still means almost half wouldn't. While two in five Americans thought Coca-Cola should use seemingly more eco-friendly packaging such as glass or aluminium for its bottles, the rest seemed less bothered. The survey did also show that two out of three believe brands such as Coca-Cola should be more responsible towards the environment, although they stop short of saying that lack of action would deter them from buying the product. Consumers' virtuous declarations can sometimes lack follow-through.

Ms Perez also stated that switching to glass or aluminium packaging would actually increase the brand's carbon footprint. According to researchers at the UK's University of Southampton, glass produces more carbon than plastic because it is mined from rare materials. And a glass bottle is forty times heavier than its plastic cousin and so requires a greater amount of fossil fuels to produce and ship.

Producing an aluminium can is also more carbon intensive than plastic; it's extracted and refined from mined bauxite ore, a complicated and energy-intensive process involving smelting at ultra-high temperatures. But it's a different case with recycled aluminium: one of those vessels has a footprint 95 per cent smaller than that of a PET plastic bottle. Unlike plastic, aluminium is not degraded when it's recycled, meaning, in theory, it can be done so indefinitely. One aluminium industry group claims that 75 per cent of all of the aluminium ever produced is still in use today, compared to less than 10 per cent of plastic (bearing in mind that mass production of plastic came in about a hundred years after aluminium). That means that 25 per cent of aluminium is still destined, along with its carbon footprint, for the bin. In the USA, several hundred million dollars' worth of aluminium drink cans alone find their way to landfill every year.

It's not just the carbon implications Coke is fretting about when it thinks about its future packaging. The raw materials for an aluminium can cost up to 30 per cent more than those needed for an equivalent-size PET drinks bottle. And that's if the material's available: the aluminium rolling industry has been increasingly turning away from can stock to the more lucrative automotive industry. It would require financial incentives to reverse that move: in other words, the price of can stock would have to rise even higher.

Glass is admittedly comparable in production costs to PET plastic. But again, the relative weight of glass puts it at a massive disadvantage to plastic when it comes to transport costs. That kind of cost increase is something that the manufacturer and subsequently the retailer would be tempted (or forced) to pass on. But would consumers stomach it, particularly if there are cheaper alternatives available?

Then there's the convenience factor: plastic doesn't break, unlike glass, nor does it dent, unlike aluminium. And, as opposed to aluminium cans, it's easily resealable. Lighter in your bag, lighter on the pocket: plastic bottles are here to stay, if soft drinks companies – and more critically their customers – have their way. As Bea Perez said, 'Business won't be in business if we don't accommodate consumers.'

But that doesn't mean Coca-Cola isn't investigating other ways to change its habits. As well as boosting the collection of waste products and the use of recycled material, they are looking at some more innovative changes.

One of the hottest new trends has been plant-based plastics. PlantBottle, for example, is a recyclable container made up of 30 per cent sugar cane, while traditional plastics make up the rest. Such bottles now make up a third of what's on the shelves in US retailers. The material has been embraced not just by soft-drink purveyors but fast-food giants, looking for greener options for the detritus that accompanies the average takeout meal.

Is it a viable solution to the problem of plastic pollution? Strong, light, versatile, clear, cheap, able to preserve contents, neither becoming permeable nor breaking down: the attributes of PET are quite a shopping list to replicate. And while poly lactic acid, or PLA – the substance found in sugar cane that suits it to being a bioplastic – ticks many boxes, it's not perfect.

Bioplastics are far more costly than their conventional rivals. A burger box made from sugar cane, for instance, is almost twice as expensive as one made from polystyrene, while a plant-based spoon can cost three times as much as a plastic one.

Moreover, their environmental credentials are far from perfect. Sure, most bioplastics can be broken down by microorganisms over time and become reabsorbed – but only if they're collected, sorted and then composted in specialist industrial composting facilities, which aren't exactly plentiful. Pop them into landfill, and they'll languish for years, releasing methane as they go, just like regular plastics.

So companies such as Coca-Cola that have turned to bioplastics have focused on encouraging customers to recycle those containers, but they're yet to be a wholesale viable replacement. The global plastic market is worth $1.2 trillion; as of 2020, the bioplastics sector was equivalent to less than 1 per cent of that. But it is projected to expand extremely rapidly as demand takes off.

Some large companies have found it easier to come up with palatable alternatives to plastic. McDonald's can boast of having just 8 per cent of its packaging in plastic form, as paper will often do the job for a burger wrapping or a straw. The ability to refill bottles means shampoo and cosmetics giant L'Oréal is aiming for 100 per cent of plastic packaging to be refillable, recyclable or compostable by 2025. In 2022, however, that figure stood at just 38 per cent. Refillable containers also rely on consumers being willing to refill and reuse packaging. And in some instances the refill containers may not be made of recyclable material, as was the case with one popular brand of washing-up liquid from another manufacturer.

There is a vast array of attempts to come up with solutions to the plastic problem, but some may not be as advantageous as they seem. Paper and compostable plastic bags, for example, might be less of a problem when it comes to littering and landfill, but they use far more energy in the production process than plastic bags so they actually have a larger carbon footprint. The same is true of single-use plastic straws versus paper ones.

This is an area where technology is developing rapidly, fuelled by the profit motive; there are both financial and reputational gains to be had. Seaweed-based straws have been developed, for example, that have the potential to be carbon neutral or even carbon negative (seaweed being a naturally occurring carbon-dioxide-capturing material). They are the brainchild of Chelsea Briganti, who founded her Loliware company in Silicon Valley, inspired by the shores she observed during her childhood in Hawaii. The seaweed is milled and ground into pellets before being formed into straw; the result is hardier than paper and only slightly more costly than plastic. Spurred on by investor interest, the company is hoping to apply its SEA Technology across more products. Other emerging plastic alternatives include the use of pea protein in a form of film.

The key to scaling up many such projects depends on funds. Investors have traditionally focused on transport and energy when it comes to green solutions; their interest is gradually turning towards packaging, inspired by some high-profile champions of the cause. Fashion designer Tom Ford is behind an eponymous prize for plastic innovations, while the Clinton Global Initiative, set up by the former US president, has showcased the likes of Loliware.

However, as businesses scramble to find cost-effective alternatives, it often comes down to governments to try to curb our appetite for plastic. There is already one major success story of reducing single-use plastics – and it's thanks to government intervention. The plastic revolution in the aftermath of the Second World War heralded the rise of the plastic carrier bag, which became commonplace in the 1970s. Cheap, weather-resistant and light; by the twenty-first century, up to 5 trillion of them were being produced every year (their ubiquity means no one can be sure of an exact number) with millions more being put into use every few seconds.

But their rise was to last less than half a century. For the typical bag ends up in landfill or – as the *Blue Planet* crew graphically revealed – choking marine life in oceans. When disposed of, a bag takes around three centuries to break down.

As awareness of the issue increased, governments started to take action. By 2018 over 120 countries had banned or levied taxes on single-use plastic bags. And where nations (including the USA) had failed to institute countrywide bans, many states and cities had stepped in with their own restrictions. By 2020, the UN estimated that they had gone from being the essential accessory of the convenience generation to one of the most outlawed products on the planet.

Even those with links to terror groups joined in: in 2018, the Somali militant Islamist group al-Shabaab, an affiliate of al-Qaeda, banned single-use plastic bags, with regional leader Mohammed Abu Abdullah hailing them as a 'serious threat to both humans and livestock . . . the waste they cause is bad for the environment'. (Some have pointed out that his concern might have been more about a possible loss of income; the group relied in part for funds on taxes paid by herders. Those taxes were paid in the form of livestock, and discarded bags were a principal source of fatalities among such animals when ingested.)

The results of the bans are a clear success. The average American still gets through two bags a day. Their use might have been restricted in California, Hawaii and New York, but cross the water from Manhattan into New Jersey and they're available with most purchases. Meanwhile the average Dane, who saw retailers prohibited from distributing the bags in 1993, uses maybe the odd one per year in an emergency.

Where restrictions are implemented, they can make a difference fast: in the UK, the introduction of a 5p charge per bag for larger retailers in 2015 saw use collapse by 95 per cent within five years. Shoppers instead turned to a reusable, thicker 'bag for life'. They're a better option – as long as they're reused, for they contain several times as much plastic as their single-use predecessors. Some retailers offer compostable alternatives or fabric totes, some of which have taken on a life of their own. London-based designer Anya Hindmarch created a cult classic with her canvas version for supermarket Sainsbury's which sported the tag 'I'm NOT a plastic bag'. It came out in 2007, paving the way for a change in attitude that would see customers become more receptive to the idea of charging for a single-use bag. It retailed at £5 and 80,000 people allegedly queued up to get their hands on one; there were only 20,000 in production. They were to change hands at £300 apiece on eBay.

In 2020, Hindmarch was back with another tote for London Fashion Week, only this time it came with the slogan 'I AM a plastic bag', for it had been scrupulously made out of recycled bottles, with a coating derived from recycled technology. It differed from its predecessor in one other crucial regard: a price tag of £695. The designer claimed that she was not making money out of them. It's a reminder that green technology can cost, particularly in the early stages.

Emboldened by its success with carrier bags, the British government extended the ban to other single-use plastics such as coffee stirrers and cotton-wool buds; the EU has taken similar action. Once again, incorporating the social cost into products has forced consumers to adjust their habits. Easy to swallow, perhaps, when the charges and items are relatively small (but still inconvenient); less so when the object concerned is far more significant – larger containers or bottles – and there are plastic alternatives available at lower cost for the less discerning.

However, for all the taste-makers, government and company initiatives at local or national level, for now, globally, the march of plastic use continues upwards.

Use in haste – wallow in waste: turning the tide on single-use plastic has proved a frustrating and sometimes fruitless challenge in the early years of the twenty-first century. Unexpected events can also set back governments' ambitions to reduce plastic waste. The spread of Covid-19 brought with it an explosion of demand for plastic PPE, for example. Admittedly, plastic pollution isn't the biggest problem facing the planet but it is one of the most visible and guilt-inducing. And the yet unknown impact of microplastics on health could be a potential time bomb. But the desire to change isn't always matched by the will to back away from a lifestyle of convenience – especially when there aren't viable or cost-equivalent alternatives.

From bans on plastic bags to deposit schemes, there are very clear examples of where a push from governments can lead to dramatic change. Alongside official penalties, there are also times when businesses will change their behaviour thanks to consumer and investor pressure. But that requires follow-through on their part. Meanwhile the search for alternatives to plastic, ones that are both environmentally friendly and affordable, continues. Innovation is happening at a remarkable pace, with business and governments increasingly realising that research and development is in their own interest.

Plastic may have been last century's miracle material but many people are increasingly of the view that it needs to be consigned to the (recycling) bin, or at least used more sparingly, if environmental targets are to be met.

7

At Work

Investments, finance and how businesses are going green

At your computer, you sift through the never-ending deluge of work emails. There's another company missive about the latest green measures and targets being implemented. You've already seen the brochures in reception and memos in the kitchen about energy-saving measures. Your organisation seems increasingly keen to prove it's cutting its carbon footprint. But is it really having any effect?

Whether a company is large or small, its managers don't just have to answer to regulators on green issues, but increasingly to customers and employees, as well as the company's owners and shareholders, and even the bank. In the financial world, where most of the funding for business – from the largest to the smallest start-ups – comes from, 'green' has become a huge issue.

Take the carbon footprint of the City of London. The alchemy of location (handily bridging the disparate time zones of the US and the Far East), language, infrastructure and regulation has made the UK the financial capital of the world. Trillions of pounds pass (electronically) through the fingertips of investors there. But size has a climate cost. If the UK's financial sector were a country, it would rank ninth in the world for carbon emissions, according to estimates from the World Wildlife Fund and Greenpeace. It's all about where the money goes: *financed* emissions. That refers to the emissions created by the companies and institutions the City funds through lending, investment or underwriting businesses. According to an analysis of 2019 data, those companies are responsible for 805 million tonnes of greenhouse gases. An increasing number of financial leaders are therefore now talking about targeting net zero on these financed emissions.

The most obvious focus – and the target of protesters' ire – are the fossil fuel giants. But it's not just about those making the energy; it's also those guzzling it. Transport, mining, heavy industry, even agriculture; financiers are increasingly held responsible for the actions of the biggest users of energy they may choose to fund. But how can they control – and change – behaviour they can't easily monitor? Why, even, should they? It's certainly not something they've cared about in the past.

Traditionally, the financial world has been about profit: getting a good return is the aim of an investor, whether they're a speculative day trader or a seasoned tycoon. Of those, perhaps the most well known – and successful – is Warren Buffett. The so-called Oracle of Omaha first bought shares aged eleven; he was filling in a tax return at thirteen. He's been at the helm of his investment company Berkshire Hathaway since 1965, and the dozens of companies he owns include Duracell batteries and restaurant chain Dairy Queen. He has amassed over $60 billion. Markets hang off his every word after a number of investments he made in the depths of the 2008 financial crisis came right.

Yet Mr Buffett has brushed off the climate implications of his portfolio. He doesn't believe it is his place to tell the companies he invests in how to behave. His organisation continues to have massive holdings in coal and other fossil fuel providers. Challenged about the implications, he argued, 'What's happening will be adapted to over time.'

But is this still the prevailing attitude across the sector? After all, ESG – environment, society and governance – appears to be at the top of millennials' investment wish list. ESG has been a buzz term for well over a decade. It's a set of guidelines to help identify green and ethical projects in which to invest. And the number of ESG investors has been steadily increasing. Micro-investing apps, for example, have engaged a new generation, particularly during the tedium of pandemic lockdown days. Over half were under forty, according to bank State Street, and they were primarily heading to funds with an ethical bent.

Warren Buffett has passed his ninetieth birthday. Perhaps he is now outdated, the voice of the past. Certainly, other big beasts in the world of finance are responding to these changes and moving with the times. At the start of the millennium, Laurence Douglas Fink was hardly a household name, even in his upscale New York neighbourhood. Tall, spectacled and softly spoken, he looks like just any other financial professional. But, within a decade, one counterpart had labelled him 'the man at the wheel of American capitalism'.

In the depths of the 2008–9 financial crisis, BlackRock, the bank he founded in 1988, was picked to manage the assets of floundering institutions such as Bear Stearns and AIG. BlackRock would ultimately bankroll a lot of Wall Street casualties, picking up the toxic assets of mortgage lenders Freddie Mac and Fannie Mae. By 2020 it had become the world's biggest money manager, with $9 trillion of funds in its grasp. That's greater than the GDP of any nation bar China and the USA. With that power came extreme influence; some people referred to BlackRock as a shadow government.

Larry Fink's every utterance was considered sacrosanct; his yearly letter to CEOs set the tone for money markets and their watchers around the globe. So, in 2020, his statement was to have a seismic impact: 'The evidence on climate risk is causing modern investors to reassess core assumptions about modern finance,' he claimed. 'In the near future . . . there will be a significant reallocation of capital.'

It was a sign that money is on the move. For many years, investors have been making big bucks from energy companies and other polluters. They're used to scrutinising financial accounts, but now they're homing in on the environmental ones. Where once the awkward questions about climate policy were the preserve of the odd 'crank' (as corporations sometimes saw them) at the annual general meeting, they're now mainstream. Investors think about the future, and for some that means low carbon. Their reasons, these days, might be as much financial as altruistic. For energy companies in particular, the looming threat of stranded assets, as we saw in Chapter 1, and the increased costs from carbon taxes, are now being factored into investors' calculations. The growing fear is that those stranded assets will mean a huge loss for investors; energy companies, for example, might see upwards of $1 trillion wiped off their value. This is one reason why oil majors underperformed most sectors on Wall Street in the early years of the twenty-first century.

Just a year after Fink's statement, at the COP 26 conference in October 2021, it was announced that 450 of the world's financial institutions, from New York to New Zealand via Costa Rica, representing $1.3 trillion of the world's capital, or funds available for investing or lending, would be gearing that money towards net zero financed emissions by 2050. It was born out of a UN-convened Net-Zero Banking Alliance, which also asked signatories to have an intermediate target for 2030, using 'robust science-based guidelines'.

It seems that many shareholders are now invested in driving through change. Capitalism finally has green's back. Or does it?

There's certainly more opportunity for investors – from the biggest to the very smallest – to influence change through responsible investing, the label applied by asset managers to funds that make a positive difference to society and the environment. There are four main strands within that.

Ethical exclusion does what it says – such funds tend to exclude industries deemed harmful, from arms manufacturers to tobacco companies. These were the first type of ethical investment funds – those that simply cut out what they deemed unpleasant. But managers' definitions of harm can vary. The so-called sin stocks represent companies occupying a spectrum that veers between the questionable and downright unpalatable;

the choice of where to place companies and invest on that spectrum is largely subjective. It's not just banks or investors that might choose the exclusion approach. Lloyd's of London, the world's biggest insurance market, conceded to years of pressure from campaigners and banned new insurance cover for coal, oil sands and Arctic energy projects from 2022, and committed to pulling out of the business altogether by 2030. But it subsequently attracted protesters outside its imposing City of London headquarters amid accusations that the moves were insufficient.

Then there are the funds that take a more thematic approach. Some invest specifically in companies that propose sustainable solutions to environmental and societal concerns. They can be quite narrowly focused, which means their returns may deviate substantially from a more mainstream fund that invests in leading companies on the FTSE 100.

There are also climate-focused funds. These will invest in the new renewable energy pioneers, as well as traditional energy providers that are transitioning to a more renewable base. After all, those traditional firms have the deep pockets and technical know-how that new entrants might not. Shareholders might also encourage them to treat outdated fossil fuel assets responsibly, rather than, say, simply selling them on.

Moving beyond simple exclusion, there is also a newer breed of investor, who looks, effectively, to influence change from within. Responsible practice means looking at how a company operates and using the levers that are available to investors – for example, shareholder votes at annual general meetings – to drive best practice. Fund managers are increasingly taking on the role of stewardship, using their financial power to engage with companies about their conduct and ESG policies.

The downside of this type of fund is that it doesn't necessarily screen out companies whose activities the fund-holder might object to, but they are still instrumental in driving through change in industries that we might struggle to do without, from aviation to construction.

Investors who opt for the last two strategies claim they can influence change better from within the room than outside it. It is why HSBC, for example, says it is persisting with its investments in fossil fuel giants, despite having been the subject of climate protests outside its headquarters. It believes it can be the influential architect of change, while providing a healthy return.

The Bank of England, too, announced at COP 26 that it would decide who it funded by looking at the carbon intensity of firms, the degree of information they published, and the efforts they made to cut carbon – past and future. It explicitly took coal off the menu. But other big polluters potentially remain. The Bank also offered up the viewpoint that while it could choose to divest, it was sometimes better to be inside the room (financially, anyway) to change hearts and minds.

For these investment giants, it is increasingly becoming a balance between reputation and financial reward. Some 650 kilometres north of London lies the UK's other financial capital, Edinburgh, home to a bank that became known for all the wrong reasons during the financial crisis: the Royal Bank of Scotland. At that time, taking advantage of its proximity to the UK centre of North Sea oil, it overtly marketed itself as 'The Oil and Gas Bank'. Fifteen years on, after a series of changes at the top, it has avoided another reputational crisis by deserting that stance (and, in a further bid to overhaul its image, is now known as the NatWest Group).

Although it still holds investments in oil and gas, they have fallen to just 0.8 per cent of its liabilities, about a fifth of what they used to be. And it has vowed not to fund such players in the industry unless they can prove they have a plan towards decarbonisation. But this is not entirely altruistic, as former boss Alison Rose was the first to admit. No rational banker would undertake the risk of being landed with stranded assets that could become liabilities. They would need a plan for how the players involved intend to maintain their revenue stream without, say, a serious foray into renewables.

This isn't just about salving a green conscience either; there is money to be made here. There is some evidence that an ethical approach to investing is financially sound. A 2020 study by analysts Morningstar found that the vast majority of ESG funds had outperformed their more traditional peers over different lifespans, possibly as they were geared more towards fast-growing tech enterprises. However, as the small print on any investment ad warns, past performance is no guide to the future.

But is all of this making any tangible difference in ethical terms to the financial sector as a whole? Not according to Tariq Fancy. Between 2012 and 2019 he was BlackRock's chief investment officer for sustainable investing. Within three years of departing, he was to become that sector's biggest critic, decrying the strategy as 'a dangerous placebo that harms public interest'. It turns out Mr Buffett is not alone in his old-school approach to investments – and that is impeding the march of the market towards green.

Fancy argued that ethical investing doesn't make any difference because companies and investors are still largely in the game to extract profit, and the biggest polluters will still find backers if they're offering up a profit. 'If you sell your stock in a company that has a high emissions footprint, it doesn't matter,' he explains. 'The company still exists; the only difference is that you don't own them. The company is going to keep on going the way they were and there are twenty hedge funds who will buy that stock overnight.' Such investors go only with business as usual. Those big investors who are backing away from certain investments, Fancy claims, are simply scared of getting their fingers burned, of being stuck with those bills from stranded assets.

Some of his former counterparts may see his views as bleak, even cynical – but this is a man who's poked the inner workings of the money machine and knows that profit is still the name of the game.

The incentive packages – and survival – of most chief executives in big companies are driven by the tyranny of delivering shareholder value, tethered to the reporting of quarterly results. That's what all sectors must bear in mind in the short term, not just energy or the very biggest polluters.

Deliver the profits, drive up the share price. And the more valuable the company, the greater the chance of being granted entry into the league table of the biggest public companies – indices such as London's FTSE 100 or 250, or the S&P 500 on Wall Street. Once in, the company will find its shares in more demand from investment managers. And if those with the deepest pockets aren't put off by a company's emissions record, what carrot is there for those executives to invest in very expensive, long-term climate policies?

The average FTSE 100 chief executive tenure is only about five years, while their net zero targets tend to be measured in excess of a decade. In 2019, for example, almost one in five of these bosses left their posts, most commonly because of dissatisfaction among shareholders at keeping up the price of their stock, or financial performance. Progress (or lack thereof) in combating climate change didn't factor in to any of their departures. Short-termism is a hard habit to break.

Tariq Fancy is also dubious of the firms that claim green credentials: 'In many cases it's easier and cheaper to market yourself as green rather than do the long tail work of actually improving your sustainability profile.' Money, he predicted, would continue to pour into 'greener' funds but it would make no difference to climate change. In other words, greenwashing would pay off to the perpetrators.

Greenwashing has certainly been an issue. Ethically minded shareholders big and small have to make sure that firms' claims are credible. In the UK, numerous companies have had ads taken off air by Britain's watchdog for claims that were judged to amount to little more than greenwashing. Recent examples include the low-cost airline Ryanair, energy powerhouse Shell, and Ancol, a maker of dog-waste bags. The Advertising Standards Authority has promised to 'shine a greater regulatory spotlight' on environmental claims in the coming years. It is also investigating how well the public understands terms such as 'net zero' and 'carbon neutral' in a bid to protect consumers.

That fundamental comprehension is central to grasping the issues surrounding climate. But even the businesses serving consumers may struggle to get a hold on terms that just fifteen to twenty years ago weren't even in their lexicons. A survey by a business lobby group found that fewer than one in ten small businesses in the UK understood what was meant by their carbon footprint, while one in five confessed that they didn't fully understand the term net zero. With a pandemic to grapple with, only one in seven had targets to reduce emissions at the time the survey was taken in the autumn of 2021, a reduction on the previous year. Almost half, however, admitted that environmental issues were a concern to their customers. But the main barrier preventing them from making their businesses more sustainable was the same as that cited by larger ones: money.

Larger companies will usually have a broader senior leadership team and will be on top of what this all means and what can be done. But that doesn't help when they decide to pull the wool over either consumers' or investors' eyes by greenwashing.

Information is key. Any economics student can tell you the basics of getting a competitive market to work efficiently is having complete information available for all participants to view transparently. Resources (money in this case) should flow to where they'll be of most effective use. A lack of information means a market simply can't function perfectly.

What can be done? Cue the government stepping in to help investors navigate their options. From 2019, all large UK corporations (those with a turnover in excess of £36 million) are obliged to record their Scope 1 and Scope 2 emissions in their annual report. These include the emissions created during transport (although only within the UK), gas combustion and indirect emissions created via electricity purchased. Big companies listed on the stock exchange must also list global energy usage.

It sounds entirely sensible, and in theory it is an important tool for those wishing to check the green credentials of where they're investing their money. But in practice it's far from easy; the data required is immense.

For example, companies have to identify exactly what is within scope, and how to measure the emissions produced at each stage of business. This is particularly fraught for complex organisations with lengthy supply chains where operations might be outsourced several times. And then there is the challenge of auditing emissions figures.

These figures also don't tell the full story. Reporting requirements don't include Scope 3 emissions, those relating to the use of a product or service once sold, or emissions from its supply chain. As seen in the case of clothing, understanding those stages can be crucial for determining and reducing an item's footprint.

The report provides a picture of only a company's current emissions. What of their future plans? How can any investor know whether they're funding a path to decarbonisation or destruction? More forward-looking money managers have already been trying to grapple with this, but a lack of data, information and a comprehensive set of standards are the biggest hurdles.

In the UK, plans to tackle this were unveiled in 2020 by then chancellor Rishi Sunak, who pledged that he was aiming to make the UK the first net zero financial centre. Sunak heralded the announcement by brandishing a version of the red box he would traditionally sport on the day of the annual Budget announcements – only this one was a shade of lurid green reminiscent of Kermit the Frog. The finance minister also decreed that all listed British firms – and all financial institutions – would have to publish plans outlining how they're getting to net zero.

Such a move would no doubt make it easier for banks to get the data and info they need to evaluate who they should be dealing with if they're truly committed to achieving net zero financed emissions. But who's monitoring the claims?

In 2022, the UK set up a task force staffed by academics, business leaders, regulators and civic society representatives to produce a scientific 'gold standard' for transition plans. The hope is to deter greenwashing. It's early days but an extension of its mandate has raised hopes it can be effective. Moreover, it's up to the investment houses to play judge and jury and, as critics have pointed out, there's nothing there to stop them from furthering 'brown investments' – those in coal, oil or gas, if they decree they tally with their own 'decarbonisation plans'.

Despite best efforts, all of this is very hard to standardise and regulate. For starters, not all businesses, in any sector, are listed on the stock exchange. That means they are not subject to these new regulations, nor to the scrutiny of activist investors or shareholders. In the UK, there are 6 million businesses but only a few thousand are listed; 99 per cent of firms are classed as small- or medium-sized enterprises (SMEs). The more enlightened banks say they're working with SMEs to help them understand and fund their transition plans. The greener the idea, the readier the cash. But again, evaluating data may be problematic.

What's more, the UK government's new requirements on information apply only to firms listed in the UK. The increasing swathes of businesses owned by private equity or overseas won't face the same obligations, nor guarantee the same level of oversight. HSBC is among the banks calling for globally consistent standards for measuring financed emissions, and also for carbon-offsetting mechanisms. This is an area where one country can't go it alone, even if it is the leader in financial services. Finance does not see national boundaries in the age of globalisation. How to evaluate the plans of companies based elsewhere?

As Tariq Fancy pointed out, the world is still awash with plenty of unethical capital. The multi-national agreement unveiled in COP 26 might represent over a trillion dollars, but that is only 40 per cent of the world's available financial capital. What of the other 60 per cent? Those investors might still be prioritising extracting profit. Developers of coal mines might not have to worry just yet.

⁓

What of the rest of us? Even if you don't consider yourself an investor, it's likely you're among them. Every person who holds an employer-funded or other private pension is a shareholder. In the UK, that adds up to £2.6 trillion worth of funds, not dissimilar to the amount of income, or GDP, generated across that economy in a year.

Pensions are hardly exciting or glamorous. For most people, their relationship with the money stashed away for retirement begins and ends with the deduction on their payslip, although some take a glance at the end-of-year statement. They then cross their fingers and hope that when they're ready to draw money out in their retirement, they have accumulated enough to allow them a comfortable lifestyle. No further thought or action required.

But it doesn't have to be that way. The average investor – people like you and me – can still influence where our money goes.

Enter Hollywood – or, rather, the man responsible for thrusting the floppy-haired charmer Hugh Grant onto global screens almost three decades ago. British film director Richard Curtis is best known for films such as *Four Weddings and a Funeral* and *Love, Actually*. He's also the man behind Make My Money Matter – a call to arms to better exercise our financial muscle.

His campaign argues that too much pension money is invested in industries – from fossil fuels to tobacco – that contradict ethical values. How about instead using your money to mirror your values, so-called impact investing? It urges people to lobby their pension providers to green their portfolio. It claims that switching a pension can be over twenty times as effective at reducing your carbon footprint as giving up flying, going veggie and switching energy providers. It's an astounding claim – and based on a study carried out by investment managers Aviva together with a data analytics company that drew on official national data. As any calculations regarding carbon footprints will involve a degree of estimation, there is inevitably some uncertainty around the results. But there are clearly gains to be had for doing a little homework into where our money goes.

Pension funds are investing for the long term. Those fund managers have the responsibility to make sure that schemes' collective pension pots are invested in such a way that doesn't leave them short when they need to pay out to pensioners. But most plans allow members a selection of funds to choose from – some riskier (but potentially more rewarding) than others. It's a case of picking priorities, and then seeing if your pension provider actually offers an option that matches them. Increasingly, they will offer at least one 'ethical' option. In 2020, there were over

300 responsible funds available to ordinary investors. They're no longer niche; the most popular funds, involving billions of pounds, are offered by the biggest players in the business.

There are certainly some catches to the ESG approach, however. For example, the fees paid on the fund to managers are typically higher on ethical funds than on traditional ones. Those managers might argue that's a result of the extra scrutiny and legwork these funds require; peace of mind comes with a cost.

What's more, there has been no standardisation across the industry on the labels applied to these funds. Digging beneath the ESG branding to discover what's actually held in a fund might take some effort, and might not be what you expect. There is no obligation on UK asset managers of funds to disclose all their holdings, so there might be the odd nasty lurking unsuspected beneath.

But that's changing. In 2022, Britain's financial regulator, the FCA, has also declared war on greenwashing. It outlined plans to label investment products based on objective sustainability criteria. It said it would impose restrictions on how terms such as 'green' or 'sustainable' can be used in names and marketing for products that don't meet sustainability labelling criteria, and force fund managers to disclose investments that customers might not expect to be held in the product.

How that will work in practice remains to be seen. But, ultimately, it should encourage consumer trust in greener financial products, and make that hour or two spent shopping around for a more ethical pension worthwhile.

Pensions aside, how can the average person get involved in channelling money in a greener form?

Investing in 'greener' government projects is one way. 'Build back better' has become a buzz phrase of governments around the world in the aftermath of the Covid-19 pandemic. Hundreds of billions of pounds have been spent on better infrastructure. Wrapped up within that, at least in the affluent West, are plans for more environmentally friendly fabric underpinning economies, from transport to homes.

In the UK, people were enticed to help fund the government spending plans, while also getting some return on their cash. Green savings bonds, in which savers' money was handed on to fund green government projects, were offered to the public.

However, initial take-up was tiny, raising less than 5 per cent of the £15 billion the government hoped in the first eighteen months. The reason was simple. The return on such bonds was far less favourable than canny savers could get for putting that cash into more conventional fixed-term accounts. Since then the return offered has been increased sharply, more likely to rival that offered elsewhere. It was a key lesson; savers weren't prepared to be penalised for worthy causes. It's one that will have to be heeded. Green bonds are increasingly a way for governments to finance their plans, and they're becoming more attractive to larger-scale investors who are cleaning up their portfolios.

Individual borrowers can also get a slice of the green action when financing their homes – at least that's the idea behind green home mortgages. Since 1992, houses in the UK have been awarded an Energy Performance Certificate (EPC) measuring the energy efficiency of a home, from A (the highest) to G. Those with the highest certification might classify for a reduction in their interest payments on a green mortgage or be offered other incentives, such as cashback. At present, they're typic-ally available for homes with an 'A' or 'B' rating – most likely new builds.

But Britain's housing stock is typically old, and among its most sought-after are lofty period Victorian or Edwardian builds. These tend to be the leakiest buildings, with draughty wooden floorboards and windows. Small wonder then that British homes are responsible for a fifth of the nation's carbon emissions.

The government says 60 per cent of all homes in 2019 were band D or lower; it aims to have them brought up to band C by 2030 where 'cost-effective, practical and affordable'. How? It wants to enlist mortgage lenders to offer lower-rate home loans to owners of less-energy-efficient properties on condition that they make the necessary improvements.

It sounds like a win-win but, in practice, might not be so simple. The cost of doing up the average sub-par home to band C is estimated to be around £8,000; it can run into tens of thousands of pounds.

By contrast, the average discount on a green mortgage com-pared to its more conventional counterpart can be just 0.01 per cent; alternatively the cashback component might be less than £200. It could be one reason why take-up has been relatively low – although the range on offer is expanding dramatically.

The incentives will have to improve if the rational home-owner is to consider it a sufficient discount to be worth the considerable outlay on home improvements, even if it will pay off in terms of lower energy bills – eventually.

What if, having done their sums, those mortgage holders decide that greening isn't worth the mortgages savings, and stick with more conventional home loans and their draughty picturesque piles? In theory, that would make their homes less desirable when they come up for resale, and therefore command a lower price – market forces penalising the less efficient.

Then the gap in price between this and a home that has been upgraded might be sufficient to prompt investment. In practice, it would also prompt outrage among those home sellers, who are typically older and, guess what, consequently more likely to vote.

This kind of market intervention might have the desired outcome but it's one that any government may baulk at.

⌒

It appears a degree of official oversight is still required – neither market forces nor consumer conscience are strong enough in any area of the financial sector to ensure industry-wide change.

In most instances, so far, authorities are relying on incentives to encourage companies to do the right thing – carrot rather than stick. But the involvement of the financial regulator in the labelling of investments is a sign of recognition that some intervention is needed.

Back to Tariq Fancy. He, after all, has been there, done that and now refuses to wear the T-shirt. If what is on offer is the 'societal placebo' he claims – making us feel better but actually delivering little change – what is the answer?

For one who was at the vanguard of the free market, his suggestion might be surprising: get the government to wade in further and right the opaque, incomplete and misleading market signals – that is, use regulation and legislation to compel companies to provide accurate information, as the UK has attempted to do. He also suggests using more widespread carbon pricing (which currently applies to only about a fifth of the world's products), specifically carbon taxes, to focus investors' minds, and again to use regulation and legislation to deter and penalise. It's back to the idea that someone, somewhere, is going to have to foot the bill to make the world greener. This time, it falls on the price tag for investors.

But such decisions are not straightforward. Carbon taxes, for example, come up against a massive obstacle, which is the same the world over: taking a slice out of voters' wallets. Indeed, sometimes the biggest opponent of doing the right thing can be political will.

Moreover, as the financial crisis has shown us, regulators can be slow to spot emerging trends and risks, and also to take action. That's not typically down to ineptitude but rather weighing up protection alongside stifling innovation and choice. Even when governments do intervene in market forces to try to ensure that money is geared towards reaching greener ends, it has to be handled with care. There can be all sorts of unintended, albeit not always unforeseen, consequences.

It remains a work in progress.

8

Time for Lunch

Balancing one of life's necessities – food – with its environmental impact

Lunchtime rolls round. You have a hard choice in front of you: a burger or a sweet potato and chickpea salad? You know the salad is better for you, and for the planet, and you've been trying to cut down your meat intake – but sometimes the temptation is just too much. And, really, how much worse can one burger be for the environment?

Our current eating habits and the way that our food is produced are both detrimental to the planet, and that's having a knock-on effect on our ability to produce food. Something has to change in the system we've created.

Part of the problem is the sheer scale of the food-production system. From the moment we abandoned our hunter-gatherer way of life for farming, humans have been looking for more efficient ways to produce food in greater quantities. That really stepped up a notch during the twentieth century, which saw a revolution in farming methods and the replacement of small-scale outfits by industrial agriculture.

As the population exploded, so too did the amount of land under cultivation for food-production purposes – from less than 10 per cent of Earth's usable surface in the 1700s to over half by 2000, for everything from raising crops and providing pasture to irrigation. The introduction of chemical pesticides, high-yield cereal hybrid species and the use of synthetic fertilisers meant that food production more than tripled between 1960 and 2020. It staved off (most of) the world's hunger pangs, allowing populations to fill their stomachs at an affordable cost. But it came at a high price for the environment.

Around 30 per cent of human-made greenhouse gas emissions are derived from the world food system, generated by everything from raising and harvesting plants, animals and animal products, to processing, packaging and shipping foods to markets all over the world. Counter-intuitive as it may seem, transport is not the overriding contributor to the environmental cost of a meal: in the EU, for example, it accounts for only 6 per cent of greenhouse gas emissions, while a whopping 83 per cent is down to the production of dairy, meat and eggs.

It's not just the emissions that have an environmental impact and endanger our way of life. As well as using up vast tracts of land, food production uses 70 per cent of our freshwater supplies for irrigation and livestock and is responsible for huge amounts of deforestation and damage to other wildlife, as well as soil degradation.

This is all complicated however by a simple fact: food production is essential. While we should certainly look at what can be done to reduce impact, we can't do so at the cost of people going hungry. Overhauling a system that people's lives literally depend on is no easy task. But it is an industry where our personal choices really can make a difference.

～

Most of us know that our predilection for meat is harming the planet. Overall, meat and dairy production accounts for 14.5 per cent of the world's greenhouse gases. In the last fifty years, meat production and consumption has more than tripled as it has become more affordable, and thanks to a growing population it's set to continue to rise. As incomes around the globe increase, it's only natural that people want to broaden their diets. But the West is responsible for the highest proportion of meat consumption – the average European eats about ten times as much as the average person in Africa.

There's an array of meat to choose from. Globally there are now an estimated 784 million pigs, 940 million cows, 1.2 billion sheep and 33 billion chickens. All those animals take up land, as well as the land used to grow feed.

The overall carbon impact of raising livestock can vary by country as not all grazing land is equal. Any resource on the planet has an opportunity cost – the benefit that is lost by not using it for a different purpose. Brazil, for example, is the second-biggest producer of beef, with massive cattle ranches, and also supplies more than half of the world's soya – a crucial source of animal feed for livestock all over the world, particularly in China and Europe. Those two factors combined have led to the destruction of thousands of square kilometres of rainforest in the Amazon, which are so important as a carbon sink for the planet, as well as devastating ecosystems and habitats that are home to rare wildlife species. One Harvard academic compared the environmental harm caused by the raising of beef cattle on grain produced in the Amazon to that of coal-fired power plants. Then there's soil degradation: eroded when forests are cleared, damaged by hooves or stripped bare through over-grazing.

Land that doesn't have an alternative use will have a far lower opportunity cost. Livestock raised in Europe or the USA tends to be a more palatable option in environmental terms. In the UK, for example, 65 per cent of farmland is suited to growing grass rather than other crops, making it ideal for grazing animals.

While all animal farming contributes to the environmental issues, it is cows in particular that have an outsized carbon footprint. Per kilogram, beef's carbon footprint is typically twice that of lamb and four times that of chicken or pork. Cows and the food and beverages we derive from them account for roughly the same amount of emissions as all the cars, trucks, aeroplanes and ships combined. And that's despite the fact beef is only the third most consumed meat, after pork and chicken. The USA holds the crown for the greatest consumption per head. The average citizen there eats the climate change equivalent every month of a return hop from London to New York.

Part of the problem is that as well as the vast resources required to raise them, cows are very gassy animals. Their belching (or enteric fermentation, to give it its formal – and more dignified – title) produces a huge amount of methane as a by-product of the digestive process. Methane is many more times as efficient at trapping heat than carbon dioxide. Sheep produce methane too, but at 30 litres a day as opposed to about 200 from a cow.

Manure also releases vast quantities of methane as well as nitrous oxide, a heady cocktail of greenhouse gases that sometimes goes under the radar. This is why discussion of the environmental impact of farming is often framed in terms of carbon dioxide *equivalent*, a unit of measurement that expresses the impact of other greenhouse gases in terms of the amount of carbon dioxide that triggers the same degree of warming. The UK's carbon footprint, for example, is about 20 per cent higher if it includes all greenhouse gases, not just carbon dioxide.

One of the ways to reduce the impact of beef is to look at ways to cut down all that methane. Given that an 8-ounce steak can on average account for 15 kilograms of greenhouse gas emissions, some of the biggest customers of beef have the greatest incentive to try to keep a lid on cows' emissions. Burger King, for example, launched a version of its Whopper made from cows fed a diet of lemongrass, which it claimed reduced methane emissions by up to a third. Another option would be using seaweed in feed, which affects cows' digestion and is said to cut their emissions by up to 80 per cent. But there's a multitude of challenges involved in applying such a dietary overhaul to the nearly 1 billion cows roaming the planet. Fundamentally, there's the issue of finding sufficient seaweed: there simply isn't the supply. Then there's persuading regulators to license its use. And it may well mean higher costs: something the more sustainably minded consumer and company might be willing to swallow – but not all.

159

Ultimately, though, reducing methane emissions wouldn't tackle the entire environmental impact of raising cows, or of course the other animals that make up total emissions figures for the industry. What we need to do is look at our own diets. A British government task force claimed in 2022 that a 20 per cent reduction in domestic meat and dairy consumption is needed by 2030, and a 35 per cent reduction for meat by 2050 if net zero emission targets are to be met. Many governments are now looking for ways to encourage consumers to make different choices. But how to convince people to eat less meat when it's become such a staple part of their diet in affluent nations?

In the UK, a group of health representatives said that carbon labelling and a carbon tax on such foods would be the most effective levers. In the latter case, they cited the success of a sugar tax, introduced in 2014, which prompted manufacturers to rework recipes to circumvent the levy.

But carbon labelling isn't that simple. In 2007, Britain's largest supermarket, Tesco, made one of its boldest commitments: to put a carbon footprint on all its products. Within a few years, those plans were dropped. Getting the necessary information, going back to every supplier and every step of the journey from farm to fork and beyond was simply too cumbersome and too costly. The footprint of even a simple piece of fruit or beef varies wildly, depending on how and where it's produced. However, advances are being made. Oatly, the biggest brand of oat-based milk, introduced carbon-equivalent labelling in 2021, and in 2023 it called for mandatory labels on all UK food and drink.

How effective are labels in influencing consumer decisions? In 2014, the UK, like some other countries, introduced a traffic-light system to indicate how unhealthy foodstuffs are. However, a red warning might not stop shoppers reaching for that chocolate (with some exceptions – Italy, for example, claimed the system had dented Parma ham sales), and to its detractors, the system had a whiff of the nanny state. On the other hand, the Hilton hotel chain has also strayed into this territory, trialling a traffic-light system on menus to denote the carbon footprint of items in some UK outlets in 2023. It's early days but it claims to have seen customers veer towards dishes with a smaller footprint.

When it comes to additional tax, academics at the University of Oxford said in 2022 that the retail price for meat in high-income countries would need to rise by up to 50 per cent for beef, 25 per cent for poultry, and 19 per cent for lamb and pork to reflect the environmental impacts of their production, be it greenhouse gas emissions, air and water pollution and loss of wildlife associated with raising livestock. It would potentially bring in billions for governments, but politicians are always loath to be seen doing anything that increases food prices, particularly those of staples, and a tax that threatened demand would be hard for food producers to swallow.

Effectively, any such extra charge would be aiming to nudge consumers into thinking of meat as a treat. But there are indications that people are already taking notice and reducing their meat intake. At-home meat consumption in the UK fell to 854 grams per person per week in 2022 – the lowest for at least half a century. There's growing interest in more 'flexitarian' diets, with a higher proportion of legumes, fruit and vegetables. Chicken and poultry consumption are growing at a faster pace than that of red meat. All have a lower carbon footprint.

Perhaps it's not only environmental concerns doing the driving here. In France, for example, people who have reduced their beef intake, when questioned, are more likely to cite health and financial concerns rather than climate change – a happy coincidence of other social costs and market forces doing the legwork. Britain's fall in meat consumption in 2022 coincided with a cost-of-living crisis; people may have been driven as much by budget constraints as good intentions. But plenty are doing it for the planet too.

To cater to this new trend, there has been an explosion of plant-based alternatives to meat in the past few years all over the world. Burgers and 'chicken' nuggets based on soy; meatballs made of pea protein or jackfruit used in the place of pulled pork; the choices are multiplying. Burger King launched a plant-based burger in 2020. It came in for criticism by vegans for being cooked alongside meat, and containing egg, but the chain's response was that it was aimed at a 'flexitarian audience', an acknowledgement in the twenty-first century that a growing audience will want a halfway house between being mainly carnivorous or solely vegetarian (or vegan).

Some of the world's biggest food companies are on to this now. Global food giant ADM is already the largest supplier of plant-based protein on the planet and has been expanding its reach, building on existing operations in China, for example, with additional investments in alternative proteins.

But has the boom in meat substitutes been overhyped? In 2019, Beyond Meat, the purveyors of burgers that 'bleed' and turn from red to brown, was valued more highly than Macy's department store on the stock market. But by 2023 that $10 billion valuation had shrivelled by over 90 per cent as buyers lost their appetites and baulked at premium prices at a time of economic stress. Sales slid by a third. Other manufacturers, from Oatly to Nestlé, pulled new vegan products from the shelves. Shoppers were opting for more traditional, wallet-friendly substitutes, such as pulses, over their more processed and pricey cousins.

But whether lentils or a bleeding burger, no plant-based option may be tempting enough to tackle the stubborn heart of the meat-consumption problem. According to a US study, 12 per cent of meat eaters in the USA account for 50 per cent of the meat consumed. For some, the habit is incredibly tough to break, and many have no interest in trying.

One area that has shown a marked difference is the dairy industry. Like meat, during the twentieth century the thirst for dairy products also rose as they came within reach of a more prosperous population. For many countries, the drinking of cow's milk is a relatively recent habit. After the rationing of the First World War, the nutrient-rich liquid provided a ready answer to a rise in malnutrition, particularly among children, and it was supplied to keep troops healthy during the Second World War. From price controls to marketing campaigns, successive governments in the West threw their weight behind promoting the consumption of dairy. The UK saw the Milk Marketing Board's catchy and innuendo-filled 'Lotta Bottle' ads in the 1980s. The next decade, the USA launched its 'Got Milk?' campaign, featuring celebrities from Kate Moss to Kermit the Frog sporting milk moustaches.

This century, however, has seen a decline of cow's milk consumption in both nations, and the closure of dairy farms (although in the USA the likes of butter, yoghurt and cheese are still on the rise). The average American drinks 440 millilitres a week less liquid milk than in 2000, while Britons drink half what they did fifty years ago. Two factors led to the revolution against milk. First: awareness of lactose intolerance. While it affects only a small minority of people in northern Europe, many started to shun cow's milk just because of the fear of the digestive and skin ailments linked to the condition. At the same time there was a growing awareness of the implications of the greenhouse gas emissions associated with dairy farms.

The range of alternatives to milk has also been growing, although many of them have been hanging in the wings for a while, waiting for wider popularity. Soy milk has been around in China for over 700 years, and almond milk has been a feature of Middle Eastern cuisine for centuries. Now, where habits are changing, food producers are pivoting to meet the demand. Visit a city-centre coffee shop in many industrialised countries and you'll probably be offered a mystifying range of options to go with your caffeine fix: soya, almond, pea, oat or coconut milk, to name a few. It's been helped by clever marketing by plant-based milk companies. The Swedish maker of Oatly has been notable for extolling the health and environmental benefits of its product, and pulling no punches when it comes to critiquing dairy, with its reference to the 'milk lobby's dirty secrets'.

Are 'alt milks' any better for the planet? On the whole, they do have a smaller carbon footprint, with some exceptions. Soy is often grown on deforested lands, for example, and a single almond seed takes over 4 litres of water to grow. But the rise of the plant-milk megabrands increasingly come with assurances of a sustainable growing environment.

That's something investors are getting wise to. Investment in protein alternatives jumped fivefold between 2019 and 2021 alone, and, according to one report, that's money well spent. Research by the Boston Consulting Group claims that each pound or dollar earmarked for expanding or improving the production of meat and dairy alternatives led to at least three times more greenhouse gas savings compared with investment in green cement technology and more than ten times as much as lower-emission cars. However, alternatives to meat, eggs and dairy products currently account for 2 per cent of protein consumption. The study was based on the assumption that the figure will rise to 11 per cent in 2035. It says that faster investment would only enhance the range and sophistication of alternatives, encouraging even faster take-up. But there's an (alternative) chicken-and-egg conundrum here. The experience of the likes of Beyond Meat demonstrates the financial risk of overhyping an alternative product, and could deter investors. But, without investment, there won't be sufficient range or quantity of products to tempt the hardiest meat eaters away.

While livestock might be the worst culprit, plant-based foods are not in the clear either. Also requiring vast amounts of land and water, they have the additional issue of pesticides and other toxic chemicals that can harm local ecosystems. Fertiliser, in particular, has a lot to answer for. It's used to make things grow, an essential way of supplying crops with nutrients. And it's used in vast quantities across the globe.

The main components in fertiliser are nitrogen, phosphorus and potassium. The first is particularly crucial to produce healthy, nutritious plants, due its role in the formation of protein. The Haber-Bosch process, which combined nitrogen and hydrogen to produce ammonia, was developed in 1913 and it enabled the mass production of commercial fertilisers. Its results were marketed with the slogan 'bread from air'. The use of those fertilisers has expanded tenfold since 1960. The results were dramatic – and not just on the field. Flourishing crops allowed the world's population to multiply from 1.6 billion people in 1900 to over 7 billion today. The biggest producers of this wonder product are worth billions of dollars.

But there's a catch: the production of fertilisers accounts for around 1.4 per cent of annual carbon dioxide emissions, more than that of many industrialised countries. According to researchers from the University of Sheffield, over 40 per cent of the carbon footprint of a loaf of bread derives from the fertiliser used to grow the wheat. Fertiliser is also a key contributor to those non-carbon dioxide greenhouse gas emissions: nitrous oxide is one by-product that can leach into the atmosphere, a greenhouse gas many times as potent as carbon dioxide. Nitrogen that escapes into the soil can promote algae growth in waterways, compromising marine life.

Those noxious gases are no laughing matter: authorities say that, globally, air pollution causes almost 50,000 deaths per day. While many sources contribute to poor air quality, it's becoming apparent that fertiliser can have a much greater impact than previously thought.

In 2014, Paris started to find itself grappling with episodes of smog. Cold weather and a lack of wind trapped a mixture of exhaust fumes, industrial pollutants and the fumes from wood-burning chimneys. At times, even its most famous monument, the Eiffel Tower, was obscured from view. It was the equivalent,

Paris's City Hall claimed, of the average inhabitant smoking eight cigarettes in a closed room per day. Drastic action was needed.

To start with, cars were allowed into the centre only on alternating days, depending on whether they had registration plates that ended in even or odd numbers. Then the worst of the diesel polluters were banned, as were wood-burning stoves. But the problem lingered. What more could authorities do? This was a country in which only 10 per cent of domestic energy comes from burning fossil fuels. The underlying cause could lie within one of France's greatest sources of pride: its homegrown food.

The French National Centre for Scientific Research found that over 60 per cent of the fine particles during Paris's 2014 smoke episode were due to ammonia. Almost 95 per cent of ammonia emissions in Europe come from agriculture, particularly from manure management and fertiliser use.

Ammonia is carried by the wind, often a surprisingly long way. If inhaled, this pollutant can be an irritant, and it can form quite a nasty cocktail when it hits cities, reacting with nitrogen oxides emitted by diesel vehicles and sulphur from power plants to form tiny solid particles. The particularly fine ones, which go by the label PM2.5, can burrow deep inside the smallest human airways. They can prompt fatal cardiovascular and respiratory disorders.

There are ways to curb the emissions produced: manure-management techniques include better storage to ensure less surface area is exposed to the air, reducing the pH of slurry and feeding the producers of said manure only the minimum amounts of protein. The type of ammonia-based fertiliser matters too. Urea is the most common due to its relatively low cost but it leaches far more nitrogen than other forms, such as those containing ammonium nitrate. Some countries, including the UK, looked at the outright ban of urea fertilisers. A more palatable option for farmers is the use of urea inhibitors alongside urea fertilisers, as occurs in Germany, which slows down the rate at which nitrogen is released.

As a major producer of wheat, France uses about 2 million tonnes of fertiliser a year. Yet agriculture has largely been left alone, while authorities have focused attention on tackling urban sources of air pollution within the boundaries of the city, by clamping down on issues such as congestion and polluting vehicles.

This is partly because many governments may be wary of going into battle with the farming industry. As President Macron found, mess with it at your peril. In 2023, after he proposed a trade agreement for more imports from South America and the curbing of farming subsidies, farmers were outraged and led protests by driving tractors into town centres and onto highways. The agricultural lobby in France is as powerful and vocal as the auto-makers are in the USA. Even the hint of reform brought farmers out to set up blockades. In reality, it was budgetary pressures, precipitated by the departure of the UK and its contribution from the EU, that brought about the proposals, but it was often blamed on environmental concerns.

However, the main reason agriculture is often left alone is because the vulnerability of farming to both environmental and market conditions means it is an unpredictable business: the wrong kind of weather can wipe out a crop and a farmer's livelihood in a matter of days, creating a shortage that pushes up prices in the market. Good weather might mean a glut, but that then forces prices down. Small wonder many governments have intervened in markets to prop up incomes and underpin supply.

The EU's Common Agricultural Policy provides subsidies to farmers for this reason, with France being the biggest recipient. That programme accounts for almost 40 per cent of the EU's budget, despite agriculture accounting for a small percentage of output. It has been ripe for overhaul for years – not least with 20 per cent of farmers getting 80 per cent of money, with the biggest benefiting the most.

Given agriculture's vulnerabilities and the amount of support it already receives, governments can be reluctant to introduce climate policies into the sector that could have a damaging effect, even if the powerful agricultural lobby could be persuaded to accept them.

As a result, while reducing ammonia emissions has been part of the EU's targets for many years, agriculture has not featured in its clean air legislation. However, as it became clear that ammonia emissions were going down everywhere apart from in agriculture, fertiliser is now being targeted at EU level. To encourage producers within the bloc and elsewhere to make their businesses greener, a key part of the EU's policy has been the Emissions Trading System (ETS). Key industries – such as fertiliser – are given a cap on the level of emissions they may produce, and they can trade allowances with other businesses to make up any deficit or offload any surplus, effectively paying more to pollute. It goes by the nifty term of 'cap and trade'.

The ETS is a form of carbon pricing: by creating a supply and demand of allowances, it effectively creates a market price for emissions. Paying for an extra allowance acts as an incentive to keep those emissions down.

But the system isn't foolproof. Why buy extra allowances when you can simply move production outside the EU, to somewhere less regulated, where there isn't carbon pricing? What's to prevent farmers from sourcing from further afield? In 2022, to counter this problem, a carbon border adjustment mechanism (CBAM) was agreed in the EU – otherwise known as a border levy – on offending items. This hybrid model would push up the price of imports so it will no longer be cheaper to source them from less regulated places. Those hoping to sell fertilisers in the EU will have to report the emissions of their goods and buy certificates matching the carbon price that would have been paid had the goods been produced in the EU. The idea is non-EU producers will need to consider measures to decarbonise in their sectors, to curb the costs of exporting to the EU. Abating the impact of ammonia – through, say, carbon capture and storage – isn't easy or cheap. The concern is that even if producers send 'cleaner' fertilisers to Europe, they could counter that by sending the cheaper 'dirty' stuff to less scrupulous customers.

European producers aren't happy. Farming organisations worry this could push up their cost of production, no matter where they source their fertiliser, and perhaps ultimately food prices, risking industrial and social unrest. It could also mean that homegrown food would be undercut by cheaper imported alternatives. To avoid that, some have been lobbying for the border levy to apply across agriculture too, to imported food-stuffs. But that would mean even more widespread increases in the cost of food.

Across Europe, many have followed the French farmers' example in response to attempts to curb emissions. Protesters in the Netherlands, Belgium, Spain and Germany have taken to the streets, dumping manure and using tractors to blockade roads, unwilling – and in some cases unable – to shoulder the costs of environmental policies. In Germany, some farmers have claimed that the phasing out of tax breaks on agricultural diesel could leave them facing bankruptcy. There's anger too at reforms to the EU's massive Common Agricultural Policy, where some of the tens of billions of euros of farming subsidies are now conditional on commitment to reduce fertiliser use.

This is a very topical issue. Russia's invasion of Ukraine in 2022 pushed up the price of key Ukrainian products, from wheat to sunflower oil, as exports struggled to leave the country under a blockade of ports. It also saw the price of fertiliser, of which Russia is a key producer, soar on global markets, due to the threat of supply disruption.

All of this triggered a cost-of-living crisis for foodstuffs globally. In France the situation was deemed so sensitive that in 2023 government ministers told companies to limit price rises, with warnings of financial sanctions for manufacturers who didn't lower prices as the cost of wholesale ingredients fell. In such a climate, there is little appetite for a green tax that would place a further burden on a population already feeling the financial pain of their weekly food shop.

This highlights a major issue with reforming the global food industry: environmental considerations cannot override farmers' ability to supply food, or a population's ability to get the sustenance it needs at an affordable cost.

ᔆ

Food security – defined as a situation where all people at all times have physical, social and economic access to sufficient safe and nutritious food that meets the dietary needs and food preferences for a healthy life – is an important global issue that every country needs to consider. Between what it produces and what it imports, does it know where its citizens' next meal is coming from?

When the price of wheat skyrocketed after Russia's invasion of Ukraine, some developing countries, such as Egypt, Benin and Tanzania, dependent on wheat imports, particularly from Ukraine, were especially vulnerable. Being heavily dependent on food imports makes countries less secure.

China, for example, houses a fifth of the world's people but less than a tenth of its farmland, so ensuring self-sufficiency in food production borders on an obsession for the authorities. Older generations may still be scarred by the memories of the Great Leap Forward that started in 1958: it promised to be a radical revolution designed to catapult the nation onto the industrial A-list. But disastrous efforts to organise vast rural communes pre-empted the Great Famine, resulting in tens of millions of deaths.

Since then, China's daily fare has proved vulnerable to global incidents: breakouts of African swine flu have affected the pig industry; a trade war with the USA led to increased tariffs on American soybeans, which are used to feed Chinese livestock; and food export restrictions imposed by Russia and Ukraine at the height of the coronavirus epidemic caused further anxieties.

China's leaders want the country to be as self-sufficient as possible. In 1996 it issued an aim to provide 95 per cent of its food, with a moderate level of imports. By and large, over the next few years, China managed it – just.

But China is still the biggest importer of food in the world – and that proportion is on the rise. Population growth might be stabilising but growing urbanisation, more upscale dietary requirements and the diversion of crops such as corn towards making ethanol for use in car fuel are all putting China's production under pressure. Moreover, just to meet the appetite for pork, it has to import 100 million tonnes of soybeans from elsewhere in the world in order to feed those pigs.

One of the most important crops it has is rice, in which it is currently self-sufficient. This is one example where the need for food security really clashes with environmental concerns.

Rice is the dietary cornerstone for half the world's population. It's also one of the more problematic foods. It produces the equivalent gases to all of China's 1,000+ coal-fired power plants and uses 40 per cent of the world's irrigation water. Bacteria in the waterlogged soil of flooded paddy fields churn out methane, particularly when the rice straw is left behind to decompose in the waters after the crop has been harvested, accounting for about 12 per cent of global emissions of methane.

One possible solution would be the intermittent flooding of rice fields, allowing them to dry out for a period rather than keeping them permanently flooded. It's a reliable way of reducing methane as well as saving water, but there are concerns it could have the undesirable side effect of boosting the emissions of nitrous oxide, that other potent gas. Vietnam, the third-biggest rice exporter, has made more climate-friendly rice part of its commitments to meeting the Paris accord targets. Measures include removing straw from the fields, using it to cultivate mushrooms and as organic fertiliser. It can earn the farmer a little extra too, but the practice is far from widescale.

More climate-friendly options are needed, as weaning growing populations off rice is just not an option. As the most affordable staple in the poorest parts of the world, mass starvation, migration and social unrest could result. In any attempt to regulate, change or improve production of such an important crop as rice, the environmental impact has to take second place to the human need for food.

This is especially true when the crop is particularly susceptible to extreme changes in the climate: in decades to come, increases in temperature could decimate yields, as well as lead to higher levels of arsenic in the soil, which would pose a health threat.

This is a growing problem across the global food system. All the way back to biblical times, food supplies have been vulnerable to the forces of nature. Joseph, him of the Technicolor Dreamcoat, managed to sustain the people of Egypt through seven years of famine through a meticulous food-management programme. Today, climate change is exacerbating the situation, as increasingly common extreme weather events – flooding, drought, extreme heat and the wrong sorts of monsoons – reduce crop yields. Warnings of famines of 'biblical proportions' are on the rise.

Overall, there is no shortage of food on the planet. Since 1960, the world's larder has been getting fuller and fuller. Food supply per head is up by more than 30 per cent. But still over 800 million people are classed as not having enough to eat. With a growing population, it is estimated that food supply must increase by 30 per cent by 2050 in order to meet demand. That will be a challenge if climate change continues to affect crop yields.

〜

So we need to protect – and even increase – yields, but we also need to address the growing environmental concerns. Catch-22. In other parts of the food industry, innovators are looking at ways to move forward: for example, modifying soybean plants so that they photosynthesise more efficiently, or using soil-scanning technology to pinpoint which areas of soil are optimal and which need some TLC.

Coffee stands only behind water and tea in the roll-call of the world's favourite beverages. It's a key export for many developing countries; in total 125 million people around the world depend on our caffeine addiction for a living. Hundreds of billions of cups are downed every day, typically thousands of kilometres away from where the beans are grown. Northern Europe holds the trophy for being the biggest consumer. From growing, harvesting, shipping, roasting and grinding, one kilo of beans can yield several times its weight in carbon. And that's before considering those ubiquitous plastic-lined takeaway cups with plastic lids.

But coffee is one of many crops that we might struggle to grow in the face of global warming. The coffee bean is a sensitive soul, thriving in moist, warm, high-altitude climates, but not if it's too warm. Rising temperatures threaten its future. In coming years, up to half the land dedicated to coffee-growing might cease to be viable.

Recently, however, the coffee research team in the Royal Botanic Gardens in Kew in London found a possible alternative. Known locally as Highland coffee, *Coffea stenophylla* is found in West Africa. The researchers stumbled on a variety in Sierra

Leone that tasted just as good in tests as more highly valued species and, crucially, could tolerate growing temperatures up to 6°C above those that other beans could withstand. It might take some time, but the scientists have high hopes that this could become a highly prized – and highly priced – commodity.

Coffee is among the top three commodities traded around the world. But unlike many traded items, coffee tends to be price inelastic – the amount we buy isn't vastly influenced by fluctuations in the price – because the cost is a fairly small percentage of our income, so we're not overly affected by price increases. As a result, from Starbucks to Nestlé, coffee companies make a good profit margin per serving, and so it's in the interests of companies such as these to ensure that coffee has a future, from bean to cup. It might mean large suppliers are incentivised to make the necessary investment to bring a new type of bean to the market.

That could be good news for growers too. In Sierra Leone, one of the poorest economies on the planet, where 75 per cent of workers are employed in agriculture, this more resilient crop could also bolster livelihoods. At the moment, it's barely a living for some: growers are very much at the bottom of the tree when it comes to sharing the spoils, while the environmental effects are felt close to home. Organisations such as Fairtrade, which works with coffee farmers to ensure they get a decent share of the takings, have also been advocating improvements including reduced use of pesticides and better water management. Pressure for more sustainable practices – for example, reforestation – also comes from the affluent customers of the bigger chains.

There's clearly more work to do in the coffee industry to bring down emissions and promote fairer conditions for all.

But a little bit of innovation means that industry could survive – and perhaps create a business model that will improve its sustainability.

༄

Of course, such a solution won't exist across the food industry. So what are our other options?

Another area where innovation might be helping to mitigate the environmental impact of our food habits is in food-waste management.

Recent studies reveal a soaring amount of food simply gets chucked away. The UN estimates that around 13 per cent of food is lost between field and shop shelf and a further 17 per cent goes into our kitchen bins. The amount of calories that get junked – largely in wealthier countries – could be enough to ensure every undernourished person on the planet is sufficiently fed.

But this is an environmental issue too: food waste in total accounts for over 8 per cent of all human-made greenhouse gas emissions. Over a fifth of the water used in agriculture is used in products destined for the bin rather than the plate. It is such a big environmental issue that one of the UN's Sustainable Development Goals aims to halve food waste by 2030.

Some of this waste occurs in the early stages: it either doesn't leave the farm to start with (as it's spoilt, sub-par or even just misshapen) or falls by the wayside at processing or retail level. More efficient farming methods could help, and better infrastructure, including roads and storage facilities, makes economic sense – an incentive for farmers and governments to stump up.

However, in industrialised countries, much waste occurs at household level. It simply gets thrown out of the fridge or cupboard. In the UK, for example, households account for 70 per cent of all food waste. In poorer countries, the amount thrown out is as little as 5 per cent. WRAP, the not-for-profit organisation that campaigns on food waste, states that there still needs to be change in consumer behaviour 'at scale'.

It's far from a throwaway issue. Remember, a third of global greenhouse gases are derived from producing our food, more than that produced by commercial air travel. Food waste has, in theory, a bigger carbon footprint than most countries, save the USA or China. Over 4 million potatoes are wasted every day in UK homes. Stopping that could have the same impact as planting 5 million trees.

The problem starts at the point of purchase. Food retailers rely on getting us to buy as much as they can. That smell of freshly baked baguettes, the premium ranges arranged at eye-level . . . just because we've clocked the marketing moves, it doesn't mean they're not effective.

Supermarkets' profit margins on selling food tend to be pretty thin, perhaps 5 per cent or so. They need customers to fill up. And what happens to the food after those customers exit the swishing doors with their loaded bags isn't their problem.

The more affluent the nation, the bigger the problem. Every year, the average American throws away more than their body weight in food – almost 100 kilograms; up to 40 per cent of what is bought can end up in the bin. That excess is proving frustratingly hard to shift.

But there's inspiration to be found elsewhere. British families cut the amount they threw out by 17 per cent between 2007 and 2021. Publicity campaigns on better storage of food, how to understand labels and deal with leftovers appear to have filtered through. There was certainly the incentive to do so: the amount of foodstuffs typically binned annually wasn't far off the average worker's salary for a week. With incomes struggling to keep up with the cost of living in the decade after the financial crisis of 2008–9, the make-do-and-mend mentality of the Second World War was back.

Reducing the amount of food we buy is one way of decreasing the resources needed to produce that food. No waste is the ideal. But there will always be occasions where food will be thrown out. No one wants food poisoning, and there are some parts, such as eggshells, that simply aren't edible. What happens to it next determines its impact on the environment.

Wasted food that goes to landfill decomposes to produce methane, that much feared member of the greenhouse gas family. For example, the vast majority of coffee grounds – around 6 million tonnes annually – end up in landfill.

To address this, separate food-waste collection – destined for the compost heap rather than landfill – has been introduced by many local authorities. That food waste is then recycled to become fertiliser (coffee grounds, for example, make for a very efficient fertiliser, once allowed to compost) or biogas. The former can be sold on to farmers, the latter to provide electricity. One UK council estimated that the food waste of its population could be sufficient to power nearly 5 per cent of their homes.

Other uses might be found for food waste. Scientists in South Korea discovered a way in which coffee grounds, once treated with sodium hydroxide, could be used to capture methane. Admittedly, those grounds absorb only 7 per cent of their weight in methane, not the most efficient method. However, it's a far cheaper way of doing so than many others on the market. So there might be a ready customer base for those dregs as the race to cut emissions heats up.

There are also a number of start-ups trying to capitalise on the business potential in coffee grounds as an untapped energy source. Leave a cup of coffee sitting around for long enough and it'll develop an oily film on top. Bio-bean, a UK-based operation, discovered that oil could be extracted from the coffee grounds and used in a biofuel. It was a neat vision: London commuters and the buses they were riding on both being powered by a dose of caffeine. The same company came up with the concept of pellets made out of grounds that could be used to heat buildings.

It was the brainchild of entrepreneur Arthur Kay. Supporting the hope that his innovation would reach industrial scale was energy giant Shell. Like its competitors, that major purveyor of fossil fuels has been keen to get behind clean forms of energy, as it attempts to spruce up its image. However, Bio-bean's plans went up in smoke – literally. A major fire at its site in 2023 saw the business, already grappling with the impact of higher inflation on its operation, collapse into administration. The company had failed to turn a profit: the economics of the most innovative start-ups can be challenging. Nonetheless, it was sold in its entirety within a couple of months to food-waste specialist enVar, which said it had hopes of introducing the product to more retailers in the future. The insolvency specialists overseeing the sale said that 'There was significant interest in the business which is testimony to the innovative product which is likely to become more and more in demand over the next few years.' There may be life in such waste still.

There are plenty more innovative projects under way – from the Scottish biotech specialists CuanTec, which is turning shellfish waste into bioplastic for food packaging, to a project looking at turning the membranes inside eggshells into wound dressings. But all of these will take time to hit the mainstream. Making the jump from bright idea to large-scale production isn't easy. Even the advent of commercial fertiliser took decades to take off globally.

The processing of food waste is, however, becoming more economically viable. Policy-makers are realising that the production of biogas could be one answer to the challenge of finding less carbon-heavy fuels. California has ambitious plans: by 2025, it intends for 15 million tonnes of organic waste to be either composted or anaerobically digested, with a view to increasing the supply of biogas.

South Korea is held up as an example of a country that recycles nearly 100 per cent of food waste, up from just 2.6 per cent thirty years ago. It banned land-filling food waste in 2005. Its stunning progress has been enabled by almost daily kerbside collections, 40 per cent of the cost of which is defrayed from the purchase of the bags (costing around 20 cents) that residents are compelled to buy to contain their waste. Almost all its discarded food is processed in into fertiliser, animal feed or biogas.

Even this success story has encountered setbacks though. As its output grew, it struggled to find farmers to take up its offer of fertiliser. Waste experts say that public procurement bodies should step in, to enable the use of fertiliser in places such as public parks, while the government has been encouraging take-up via urban farming programmes, which include composting courses and project grants. Meanwhile, the viability of using recycled food waste as animal feed was undermined by diseases such as avian flu and African swine fever, and its production of biogas has been hampered by capacity constraints, but it is developing new facilities to greatly enhance that.

Such innovations in recycling, as well as in farming and production, are going to be key to feeding world populations sustainably in this century. The challenge will be to make them work economically in a highly price-sensitive area. The economics of food supply are all important, trumping the environment in most cases.

Not eating is not an option. But the need to tackle the climate impact of our foodstuffs is mounting. It's in the clear interests of everyone – producers and consumers – to do so. Especially because, unlike many other topics in this book, this particular industry is not just a major cause of climate change, but also feels the brunt of its force, sometimes in the most brutal way.

9

Making a Purchase

The hidden cost of how we pay

On the way home, you make a quick detour to head into a shop to pick up some essentials. There's a queue; the customer at the till is paying in cash, the sales assistant doling out change. It's been a while since you have had money weighing down your wallet. These days it's just a quick tap with the plastic and done; since the Covid-19 pandemic, contactless rules. And it turns out that change could well have worked for the benefit of our planet.

Cash, card or a swipe of your phone; it can take only seconds. You might think that simple transaction couldn't possibly have added anything to your emissions tab. But while the payment sector certainly isn't competing with energy generation, transport or industry for its carbon impact, it does have one. Overall estimates are hard to come by, given the myriad methods of payment, and not many processors estimate their footprint. But just take our plastic habit: 25 billion card trans-actions occur in the UK every year, leaving 1 million tonnes of carbon dioxide in their wake, partly thanks to the manufacture of the cards themselves but mainly due to the manufacture and energy costs of the payment terminals, which themselves have a limited shelf life.

The (mostly) good news is that this is still an improvement on the past, and there's a growing awareness of a need for greener payment methods in the future, perhaps especially with the rise of cryptocurrencies such as bitcoin.

Let's start with cash, our oldest form of payment. Is it the least environmentally friendly? The first coins used as a method of payment consisted of an alloy of silver and gold. Their modern counterparts are made of much cheaper, more readily available metals, with of course paper notes playing a part. But all physical money has an environmental cost, from the mining of materials, the destruction of trees, transport and distribution, right through to its disposal.

Mining accounts for almost a third of the cash carbon foot-print. But the bulk of the footprint is down to the way it's dispensed. Running an ATM takes considerable energy. One study estimated that each wad of notes typically comes at a cost of 4.6 grams of carbon dioxide. The industry argues, how-ever, that each ATM withdrawal typically funds five different payments, implying a relatively low footprint for cash, per transaction at least.

What of the making of banknotes themselves? Many coun-tries are ditching the paper option and turning to polymer instead. Australia did so back in the 1980s; the Bank of England issued its new £5 and £10 notes in 2016 and 2017 respectively.

Polymer notes are billed as safer, stronger and cleaner than their predecessors. They are more durable, less prone to carry germs and won't have to be replaced as quickly. The Bank also claimed that the notes had a reduced carbon footprint of between 8 per cent and 16 per cent compared with the paper versions.

Payment, then, with less guilt attached? It's debatable. A separate comparison by Evergreen Finance London, using the Bank of England's data and industry numbers on usage, claimed that for the average number of notes used by one person each year, the production and use of the new polymer £10 notes releases 8.77 kilograms of carbon dioxide across their life cycle, almost three times more than previous paper notes. While the Bank of England had looked at the circulation of 1,000 banknotes over a decade, this later study also looked at the number actually used by a person, how they're made and, crucially, the number of exchanges they go through. On that basis, polymer notes were more damaging – even allowing for a longer lifespan.

Who's right? With so many different factors to consider, it's hard to say, but perhaps the answer is becoming less relevant in an era when the overwhelming proportion of payments in the UK are cashless.

Cash use has been declining for a while now. Card payments took over as the dominant form of payment for retail in 2016. By 2021, 85 per cent of payments were made electronically, either as card payments or bank transfers. Convenience and the march of technology played a role, heightened by the experience of the pandemic. The UK finance industry forecasts that by 2031 only 6 per cent of payments will be in cash.

But that doesn't sound the death knell for cash. Many people, particularly the elderly and those at the bottom of the income scale, rely heavily on cash. A study for the financial regulator in 2022 found that 6 per cent of British adults relied entirely on cash for payments, rising to 9 per cent of those in vulnerable circumstances. As our payment infrastructure moves to exclude cash payments, there's a real concern they could be left behind.

Globally, cash still accounted for 16 per cent of transactions in 2022, but it varies substantially by country. While it's 12 per cent in the USA and 10 per cent in France, it can be much higher in some developing countries: over half of sales transactions in Thailand are in cash and as much as two-thirds in Nigeria. Many countries are seeing a decline as other payment methods become more popular and populations more affluent. In some nations – Brazil and India, for example – governments are actively encouraging a shift away from cash, not least to make it easier to track economic activity and collect tax.

It might sound a bit old-fashioned, but some places do rely heavily on another form of paper payment: the cheque. While most of us in the UK are probably uncertain where our cheque-book is, given how rarely we use it, over half of Americans wrote at least one cheque in 2022. According to one source, that's 15 grams of carbon dioxide per cheque, due to the printing and processing of the payment. Factor in the 2.3 billion cheques collected each year and it quickly adds up. But globally the cheque is on the way out; like cash, it's given way to the popularity and convenience of credit and debit cards.

Billions of card transactions – the most popular method of payment – take place in the UK every year. Is the move to cards that much of an improvement for the environment? There's the water, plastic and transportation involved in manufacturing a card, and then the footprint involved in sending it to the customer, and building and powering payment infrastructure, such as the contactless payment terminals. That last one is the biggest contributor to the estimated 3.78 grams of carbon dioxide each card transaction accounts for. One study compared the carbon footprint of making a card and that of producing cash, claiming the carbon emissions of one card were equal to that of thirteen banknotes. Of course, over its lifetime one card will be responsible for far more transactions, and so is likely to be the less harmful option. And the industry argues that the advent of data sharing, for example via the Open Banking mandate in Europe, has streamlined the payments process, reducing its carbon footprint.

Online payments have the potential to reduce emissions drastically. Whether you use virtual cards, online wallets or apps such as Venmo, the payment takes just a few seconds to make, and more widespread adoption could cut emissions in the sector by 80 per cent. It could be argued you should take into account the manufacture of the smartphone, which would obviously wipe out most of the benefits. To compensate for that, a phone would have to be used for over three decades; for most people, it's more like two or three years. But considering the fact that very few people will have bought a phone specifically for this purpose and will be using it for plenty of other things, perhaps that's an unfair burden to place on this method of payment.

With digital payments on the rise, we are, arguably, making some steps in the right direction. But not every innovation in the world of payments has factored in the environmental cost. Enter bitcoin.

Even digital forms of payment are beginning to feel outdated in the race for new forms of currency in the digital age. Bitcoin has fast become the byword for cryptocurrencies, being the most prevalent of its type. It rose out of the ashes of the financial crisis, the episode that brewed not just financial havoc but a mistrust of the wider system.

Bitcoin was based on a concept published in a 2008 white paper by a shadowy figure, or figures, who operated under the pseudonym Satoshi Nakamoto. It was intended as a peer-to-peer cash system, with coins transferred at a touch of a button, and stored digitally in wallets. It was not backed by governments nor regulated by them, which became part of its attraction – and its drawback. It quickly garnered a reputation for being the favoured means of currency for money launderers and other wrongdoers. With a maximum supply of 21 million coins, its value fluctuates madly, rendering it more of a speculative asset rather than a means of payment. Although there are some instances where bitcoin is accepted as payment, they remain relatively sparse.

Being widely and readily acceptable is one of the basic functions of money, and in this bitcoin and its counterparts diverge somewhat from more traditional forms. But more problematic in environmental terms is that the coins need to be digitally mined, and that's leaving quite the carbon footprint.

Whenever a financial transaction takes place, the person doing the spending has to be verified as the owner of the funds and completion of payment has to be recorded in a database. For a conventional payment, that happens centrally within a bank. With bitcoin, that process is done by miners, who record the transaction in a blockchain ledger or database. They authenticate batches of transactions on computers through mathematical puzzles. Whoever solves the equations first and adds it to the blockchain is rewarded with a digital coin. That's why they're known as a 'proof of work' coin. The puzzles have to be complex enough to prevent hackers seizing control.

As bitcoin's value has risen, so has the thirst for mining, and the more complex the equations have become. The faster the miners can provide answers and a series of random numbers to the equation, the greater the likelihood of releasing the coins.

As a result, mining is no longer the work of the stereotypical geek in the bedroom – no ordinary desktop PC is likely to be able to cope with the demands. Increasingly, it requires roomfuls of powerful, expensive and highly specialised machines, going at full tilt. Consequently, the entire process becomes incredibly energy intensive.

Bitcoin accounts for around 80 per cent of the market of proof-of-work coins, out of a population of around 500 types of coin. According to estimates from the University of Cambridge, bitcoin in 2019 consumed more electricity than the economy of Sweden or Norway. A study by Italy's central bank said that the Eurozone's own payment system had a carbon footprint 40,000 times smaller than that of the best-known digital currency. Bitcoin has faced accusations that it could account for a substantial part of global warming within three decades.

It's not the just amount of electricity consumed, but the type. China is not just the world's workshop and factory, it's also the dominant source of bitcoin mining, accounting for about 65 per cent. And in that country coal still accounts for the greater part of the energy mix. A study found that three out of four miners questioned claim to use renewable energy as part of their power source but that is at odds with a country where less than 40 per cent of energy consumption comes from renewables.

The issue was brought to the world's attention by a man who also pioneered premium electric vehicles and, more controversially, civilian space travel. Elon Musk, the boss of Tesla, is known for his social media antics, but his pronouncements in May 2021 that his company would not be taking bitcoin as a form of payment wasn't just an attention-seeking stunt (although it was enough to send the value of the crypto asset plunging). He argued that there was simply too much fossil fuel involved in the creation and movement of the digital currency. He later tweeted that Tesla would accept payment in bitcoin 'when there's confirmation of reasonable (~50 per cent) clean-energy usage by miners with positive future trend'.

His high-profile move itself was enough to highlight the reputational risk to bitcoin, prompting swings in its value and making other companies think twice about accepting it, incentivising behavioural change from miners.

That's not to say, however, that bitcoin has been cast out in the cold following this public naming and shaming. Within a couple of months of his initial comment, bitcoin had regained its value. After all, those who are in it for speculative purposes might not have the same concerns. And indeed, Tesla's accounts for 2023 revealed it retains one of the largest bitcoin holdings of any publicly listed company.

The complexity of mining makes it hard to get accurate comparisons of the environmental impact of different cryptocurrencies. Going on what we do have, none of the highest profile of the initial wave come out particularly well but some estimates put bitcoin as the worst offender, with Ethereum slightly less damaging. Dogecoin, whose founder admitted to not considering the issue of emissions originally, cut emissions by a quarter in 2022 after teaming up with Elon Musk to make its system's transactions more efficient.

The Ethereum blockchain system has also enabled the growth of non-fungible tokens or NFTs, the proof of ownership of a piece of digital art. A way for artists to underscore the originality of their creations and harness income, or another burden on the environment? The creation of the work itself may not be carbon intensive. But when an artist 'mints' an NFT of their work as part of the sales process, it creates an entry into a digital ledger, a blockchain. Those run mainly on the Ethereum blockchain system, and the use of a blockchain to mint an NFT can use more electricity than an average American household uses in a month. For an artwork you can't hang on a wall, it's hugely energy intensive.

Meanwhile, others have been trying to muscle in on the crypto rush. In 2019, Facebook (now Meta) caused the world to pause when it announced that it was joining up with over twenty-five of the biggest names in payments – from Visa to MasterCard and PayPal – to launch the Libra Association; the aim was to launch a digital payment platform, and a digital currency, whose value would be linked to that of leading currencies. In other words, it would be a so-called stablecoin, rather than an investment asset.

Outrage was soon to follow. With Facebook having over 2 billion monthly active users, governments feared it would give one company, and its associates, too much power, enabling them to create a rival to national currencies, and allow the potential for abuse of users' data. There were concerns it would be used for fraud and money laundering. Libra's backers were quick to dissociate themselves from the project, and over the next couple of years it was significantly watered down. But even in a slimmed-down form, there was little in the way of questions being asked about the environmental credentials of this new stablecoin.

What we do know is that an established brand such as Facebook has come under immense pressure to reduce its carbon footprint, and has done so, with emissions reduced by over 95 per cent by introducing various measures such as a large-scale switch to renewable energy. With big tech eager to burnish its clean-living credentials, net zero data centres are becoming a way of business. In this sense, at least the new arrivals might raise the bar on environmental issues.

The emergence of Libra also gave governments and central banks around the world a sense of FOMO. In 2021, the UK's Treasury and the Bank of England announced they were looking into the possibility of a central-bank digital currency. They quickly took to using the shorthand CBDC to get round the unwieldy title, but even before a decision had been made whether it would become a reality, that currency had been dubbed Britcoin. The idea was that it would be a stable currency to rival those put out by private providers, which would also be regulated, and, unlike bitcoin, backed by a central bank.

By the central bank's admission, it is many years before this may become a reality and in the meantime there is much to be hashed out. But among the questions already being asked was how it would compare in environmental terms.

The Bank's answer is that not all blockchain processes and centralised ledgers have to be as energy intensive as those involved in bitcoin. Saying 'let's not throw the blockchain baby out with the bitcoin bathwater', the Bank points out that many of the new technologies being developed are thousands of times more efficient when it comes to processing transactions.

It also flagged that authorities from the G7 group of richest nations had pledged that energy efficiency should be a core consideration for CBDC design, and that the very data provided from such a currency would provide insights that would allow improvements in energy efficiency.

Digital assets might have been around for over a decade but government and central banks are still in their early exploratory stages. However, with the scrutiny of the public, they might be able to go where the pioneers of cyber assets didn't, providing a safe, stable and carbon-friendly form of digital currency.

Already, there are alternate forms of digital currency being explored. Chia relies on a 'farming' process using hard drives, a form known as 'proof of space', rather than the mining, or proof-of-work concept, used by bitcoin. It doesn't rely on vast computer processors and can be farmed on the hard drives of laptop or desktop computers. Even so, that feeds the demand for hardware, and contributes to the creation of that twenty-first-century blight: e-waste, which, as we saw in Chapter 3, is already substantial.

Meanwhile, SolarCoin was created to reward generators of solar energy by giving them free coins in return. Likewise, Bitgreen incentivises green behaviour by rewarding activities such as carpooling.

The evolution in the payments industry has been driven by cost and convenience, for both consumers and the industry. Regulatory issues aside, to protect customers and uphold the credibility of systems, there has been little official intervention. But the changes haven't always been matched by rapid progress in environmental credentials; those tend to fly under the radar.

Digital currencies and bitcoin might feel a long way from becoming a mainstream form of payment, but we should be planning ahead to ensure they're not an environmental step backwards when they do arrive.

10

Heading Home

Living in a world of concrete and steel

A s you drive home, you get stuck in a traffic jam at temporary lights. There's some sort of roadworks going on – the whole area feels as if it's under construction. There's another tower block being built there, scaffolding all over the one across the road. Everywhere you look, more concrete and steel is going up around you.

All over the world, governments and businesses that are trying to construct a prosperous economy may at some point turn to bricks and mortar, the physical act of building to stimulate the process. Each £1 spent on construction by the state can, typically, generate up to £2 towards the country's income, or GDP. When the cranes go up in a city, it's a sign of confidence, growth, hope for the future. And the chances are, wherever you are, all those new buildings will be made of concrete and steel. These are the foundations of economic development. From offices to schools, homes to hospitals, railways to factories, they are the essential components of the infrastructure that improves our way of life. No town planner or policy-maker can do without them.

Discussions of how to make buildings greener usually focus on increasing their energy efficiency, but the very fabric of their construction also has an environmental impact. Although relatively under-reported, concrete and steel are high on the list of climate killers. A report for the UN in 2019 claimed construction accounted for almost 40 per cent of energy- and process-related emissions. There is a huge environmental cost to their use.

Demand from customers around the globe means business is booming. Many governments' Covid-recovery stimulus packages contained plans for traditional infrastructure projects, a sure-fire way of boosting and quickly increasing jobs. Each £1 billion spent typically creates work for thousands. But such projects require vast quantities of materials. As the world continues rapidly urbanising, demand will increase: by 2050, 70 per cent of people around the world will be living in cities, twice the figure for 1970.

What's more, as industries around the world look towards a greener future, steel is going to be instrumental in the decarbonisation process: it is the essential material for wind turbines, for example, and used in the frames for solar panels. Concrete is also intertwined in the physical structures needed for a lower carbon future, from nuclear plants to towers for wind turbines. It seems that there are few other materials that can compete, particularly for affordable use at scale. For now, both are here to stay.

∽

For centuries, concrete has been used to project success and power, from Rome's Colosseum to the 163-storey-high Burj Khalifa in Dubai. The former, completed in 80 CE, is testament to the resilience and durability that the material provides. Today, 30 billion tonnes are used every year.

The key ingredient in concrete is cement – it's hardly glamorous or exciting but it is the second-most-used product (after drinking water) on the planet. Cement is made by pyroprocessing: roasting raw materials such as limestone at ultra-high temperatures in a kiln to produce clinker, small lumps of which are then finely ground and combined with other substances. That cement is then mixed with rocks of differing sizes to form concrete. Cement typically makes up less than 15 per cent of concrete, but it accounts for the overwhelming majority of concrete's carbon footprint, thanks to the burning of limestone.

Cement currently accounts for 7 per cent of global carbon dioxide emissions and about a quarter of all industry carbon dioxide emissions. Tackling cement, therefore, has to be built into any plans for a lower-carbon future; the industry must cut its emissions by a sixth if the terms of the Paris Agreement are to be met. As pressure grows from policy-makers and investors, the more forward-thinking cement-makers are scrambling to avoid their industry becoming the next climate pariah and risk being left with stranded assets.

Most modern cement plants are already focused on energy efficiency – after all, it's typically cost-efficient too – but it is an energy-intensive process, and the high temperatures required mean that there isn't currently a clear alternative to fossil fuels. Studies have been carried out to test the feasibility of replacing them with a mix of hydrogen and biomass, but there is still a long way to go. Other ways to reduce cement's carbon footprint must be found.

One option would be to find alternatives to clinker, which would reduce the amount of limestone being burned. It is clinker that gives cement its characteristic strength, but it can be substituted in part with waste materials such as blast-furnace slag – a by-product of steel-making – and coal ash from coal-burning plants. That switch has actually been happening for decades, initially propelled by costs. While it's long been acknowledged that this has the benefit of diverting such waste from landfills, it's relatively recently that these alternatives have been marketed as 'green products'.

There's an obvious flaw in this plan, though. With coal-fired plants themselves being phased out, coal ash is becoming increasingly scarce. As industries across the board look to decarbonise, both types of waste materials are becoming more expensive and fought over; they're no longer necessarily the cut-price alternative.

Another option being explored is carbon capture and storage (CCS). A chemical gas company in California has been injecting carbon dioxide captured from the atmosphere into concrete in an attempt to lock it in. Viability, including cost, at an industrial level, is yet to be determined but it is an alluring solution – and not just for this industry. Researchers at London's Imperial College argue that the most effective path to decarbonisation is to make the use of CCS technology the norm, and the International Energy Agency has factored it into its plans for how the world will move towards net zero in the coming decades.

The path to rolling the technology out at scale has not been smooth. However, the greenlighting of the first industrial-scale CCS plant, the HeidelbergCement Norcem plant in Brevik, Norway, supported by government investment, is promising a breakthrough. It intends to be fully operational by 2024. Such developments could help industries such as cement-making to deal with at least some of their emissions.

It doesn't look as though there is any real large-scale alternative to cement or concrete in the short term. What of steel?

The blast-furnace method of making steel was first developed in 1856 by Henry Bessemer, a British inventor who registered over a hundred patents. Of all those inventions, it was this process that fuelled the Industrial Revolution, making steel available in industrial quantities at an affordable price. One of the most innovative, flexible, versatile and cheap alloys, steel made the modern world as we know it; it's used in housing, transportation, industrial manufacturing, automobiles and infrastructure.

To make steel, iron ore is heated and melted in huge blast furnaces where the impurities are removed and carbon added. A key component is metallurgical or coking coal (different from the thermal coal used for fuel), which is heated to above 1,000°C to make the coke used to purify the metal in the furnace. Given how energy-intensive the process is, successive generations have sought to make it more efficient but, even so, every tonne of steel produced in 2018 emitted on average 1.85 tonnes of carbon dioxide. That accounted for 8 per cent of global carbon dioxide emissions.

There's a conundrum here: steel has an important part to play in the green transition, yet its manufacture relies on a coal product – a key reason why those in that part of the coal-mining industry (which is based largely in the USA, Canada and Australia) argue that it would be counterproductive to cut off their funding entirely – at least until an alternative method of production goes mainstream.

One of those alternatives is melting down scrap steel in electric-arc furnaces, which tend to be smaller, more flexible and, crucially, emit far less carbon dioxide than their blast counterparts. The steel trade association says utilisation rates could rise to a third globally by 2025, but it's still a far from comprehensive answer: there is a limited supply of scrap steel, and the furnaces are not viable at the scale needed for, say, the automotive industry. To be consistent with 1.5°C warming, Global Energy Monitor, a Californian think tank, has calculated that electric-arc furnaces would need to account for over half of global steel-making capacity by 2050.

As with cement, the industry is also looking at other ways to power the coal-guzzling blast furnaces. Steel-makers in Europe are leading the way, given that they are under pressure to reduce their carbon footprint to meet the EU's Green Deal goal of eliminating net-greenhouse-gas emissions by 2050, and to comply with emissions trading schemes.

SSAB, a Swedish group, is staking its bet on hydrogen to remove fossil fuels from every stage of the steel-making process. But it reckons that this route will initially be at least 20 to 30 per cent more expensive than using a blast furnace. However, number crunchers at McKinsey say that as interest and investment multiplies, the cost of green hydrogen should drop sharply (see Chapter 4). By 2050, with increases in scaled hydrogen production and carbon taxes, they are hopeful that there will be competitive green options for steel-makers. But that's uncertain. And still some way off.

In the shorter term, Europe's biggest steel-maker, ArcelorMittal, says it has the technological know-how to eliminate greenhouse gas emissions by 2050. It is, for example, building a facility in Belgium that will turn toxic waste wood into 'bio-coal', with a lower carbon dioxide footprint, to replace a portion of the regular variety in blast furnaces. It is also experimenting with carbon capture at that site. But it's warned that decarbonising its operations would cost up to €40 billion, for which it has called for public funding and policy support. ArcelorMittal executive chairman Lakshmi Mittal stated, 'The support that the EU and member states can give to ensure we have a well-designed policy to make large-scale, competitive, carbon-neutral steel-making a reality is critical.'

If governments are reluctant to cough up, that would pass the bill on to customers. And price is the most sensitive area in steel-making. The West already struggles to compete with the world's biggest producer: China.

Construction has played a crucial role in China's transition from developing nation to bristling superpower, at home and abroad. After it started to embrace capitalism in the 1980s and 1990s, its development mantra has been 'build, build, build' – offices, factories, workshops – and the backbone of that has been made literally of steel and concrete.

At the height of its building boom, around a third of China's economic growth came from its property sector. According to think tank Chatham House, China devoured more cement in the three years between 2010 and 2013 than the USA did in the entire twentieth century. The construction boom gave rise to tower apartment blocks and shopping centres as the country urbanised: the proportion of China's population living in cities doubled between 1998 and 2020. It meant that Chinese real estate was rumoured to be the largest commercial sector on the planet at its peak in 2021. That bubble subsequently burst as developers buckled under the weight of new state-imposed limits on debt, but the country still accounts for half of the world's cement demand.

Since 1990, China has been responsible for some three-quarters of global cement production. Six of the ten biggest cement-makers in the world are Chinese. By 2018, China had 49 per cent of the global market in steel too. While these industries were powering economic development at home, they had also become entwined with railways, cars and buildings thousands of kilometres away. Both materials were crucial to China's overseas plans, building infrastructure such as airports and dams as part of its Belt and Road Initiative (BRI), a vast investment project stretching from Africa to South Asia. The overland routes connecting China to Europe through Central Asia, and going on to South Asia and South-East Asia, form the Belt, while the Road, contrary to its name, is the maritime link between China and key ports. It was billed as providing development opportunities for low- and middle-income countries, while also providing opportunities for Chinese companies and facilitating the flow of the raw materials they need. Crucially, it was seen as cementing China's global economic power.

Given the importance of the steel industry to its ambitions, the government subsidised it heavily. It was priced to undercut the competition, leading to a slump in global steel prices with consequences that reverberated around the world. Other countries found it increasingly hard to compete: in the USA, it sealed the fate of the already declining Rust Belt states, with steelworks lying empty and workers forced to accept a career change. Cheap, plentiful Chinese steel was the trigger that set off a trade war with the West in 2018, resulting in tariffs being slapped onto millions of dollars' worth of Chinese goods by President Trump and similar retaliatory measures imposed by Beijing. The losers were customers, forced to pay higher prices.

'Build, build, build' might have been the mantra, but going all out for growth meant a cost for China. In 2020, the country produced around a billion tonnes of steel, which accounted for a fifth of its coal use.

In March 2021, pollution sat centre stage at the annual meeting of China's national legislature, so much so that a curb on steel production was imposed. It was decreed that production in 2021 should be no higher than it was in 2020. But it came with unacceptable consequences: there was immense resistance from the provinces and industry on the grounds of economic security. The views of China's environment ministry remain at odds with those of its industrial planners.

Just as in the glory years of the USA's Rust Belt, China's steel-making industry supports many jobs – millions of them, in fact. Where production had been cut, many were working on reduced hours, and that had a knock-on impact on the construction industry and local governments. The latter have been big beneficiaries of China's 'build, build, build' programme, due to the taxes collected on land sales.

The pause, in the end, was short-lived. In the first half of 2021, China actually accelerated its expansion of coal-powered steel mills, with eighteen steel-making blast furnaces announced.

So much for stepping down the industry. The siren call of global market domination achieved by keeping prices down – whatever the costs – takes precedence over environmental considerations. Some argue the new plants will be more efficient and greener. The industry has pledged to cut emissions by 30 per cent from its peak by the end of the decade, in part by replacing hundreds of millions of tonnes of ageing capacity with newer and cleaner equipment. But the new plants also tie steel-makers' fortunes to coal for longer by extending the use of blast furnaces. The impetus to move towards greener steel has been increased by a forthcoming tax to be imposed on carbon-heavy imports by the EU and the UK from 2026, with an expectation that other countries may follow. China is still a way off from declaring that the air pollution is problematic enough to slap a carbon price on its polluting heavy industry. Demand for steel is not going to collapse any time soon, particularly as countries around the world look to shore up their physical infrastructure after the initial body blow of the pandemic.

The irony is that China was sitting on a vast overcapacity of buildings, from offices to shopping centres, in many of its cities. But tried and tested habits are hard to break. It can be hard to move away from building as a prop for economic growth, even once a country becomes more prosperous.

Japan is often touted as the prime example of this. In the aftermath of the Second World War, with its cities physically shattered by nuclear attack and its economy ravaged, construction was a way of rebuilding the nation. The country entered a state of what was labelled *doken kokka*, or 'construction state', to drive its transformation. Once cities were rebuilt, the government turned its attention to railways for bullet trains, expressways and stadiums, turbo-boosting it into the economic premier league. It was spending on building as a way of creating jobs, stimulating the economy and improving its citizens' way of life. But it was difficult to stop. The government found itself compelled to keep throwing funds at new, increasingly less productive projects to maintain the momentum of growth, creating costly white elephants of the twenty-first century, such as bridges that lead to almost nowhere (nowhere that anyone wants to go to, anyway).

In China, some of its shopping centres and apartment blocks may increasingly lie empty but it's hard to turn off the taps in an industry that employs over 50 million people and once propelled growth. Now, though, the use of construction to drive expansion appears to be turning a corner; officials might say this is by design, but others suggest it's the overdue bursting of a bubble.

Evergrande is China's second-biggest property developer, claiming to own more than 1,300 projects across the country. Its founder was once one of the richest men in Asia. Riding the wave of its success, the Evergrande Group diversified. It makes electric cars, foodstuffs, offers financial services and is part owner of one of China's biggest football teams, Guangzhou FC. Yet saddled with more than $300 billion of debt, it fell foul of rules introduced in Beijing that limited the amount companies could hold, prompting it to flog properties at a deep discount. It then struggled to meet its interest payments. It filed for bankruptcy in New York in the summer of 2023 to protect its US holdings. Its share price had already collapsed, hitting millions of investors, from middle-class households to the biggest banks. The unmanaged demise of the group itself would risk being disastrous, both for suppliers and for China's wider financial system.

The government's plan to restructure the economy involved curbing the construction sector, pivoting it away from an outdated reliance on building and speculative projects via regulation. But this sort of correction threatens the very foundations of China's economy. Many analysts speculated Evergrande would be 'too big to fail', that the state would step in to at least prop up a shell of what the company used to be. Either way, the shift might curb China's appetite for concrete and steel, on home turf at least.

China continues to export its dreams for growth and industrial prowess, but its Belt and Road projects in poorer countries have run into issues too. It stands accused of building several white elephants, making full use of that steel and concrete elsewhere, and some of its clients – from Kenya to Laos – have struggled to pay back the loans involved. Others are already picking up some of the environmental tab for China's ambitions. A World Bank report found that the large infrastructure projects under the BRI expose the countries and local communities involved to environmental damage, including water pollution and soil erosion. That's before even considering the carbon implications of the materials involved, as China is setting up dozens of concrete factories in overseas countries to complement the BRI projects. It has prompted mutterings of climate colonialism among some academics in the USA: exporting poor environmental practices abroad under the guise of helping the recipients to develop.

❦

An intense relationship with concrete has often typified the move to an advanced economy. In recent decades, its production has outstripped that of steel threefold as more countries lift their people out of poverty, paving the way to a more financially secure existence.

By 2060, the amount of built floor space across the globe is set to double, bringing economic and physical benefits (swap a mud floor for a concrete one, for example, and you slash the incidence of parasitic diseases). Chatham House predicts that economic development and population growth will push global cement production up by another billion tonnes per year, from current levels of just over 4 billion tonnes, as developing countries look to raise their infrastructure to the norm elsewhere. India and Indonesia, for example, are just embarking on a concrete-intensive chapter of growth, with construction sites in Delhi already clogging the air with fumes. India is coming up behind China in the production stakes, and the demand from customers around the globe looking to emulate China's success is booming.

The lack of affordable, environmentally friendly alternatives to concrete is problematic. There are plenty of customers who have yet to reach peak demand who could ask why they should pay more than their richer counterparts simply to attain the same standard of living, when they are currently less likely to be able to do so.

It's the developing countries, of course, that are most at risk of economic damage wrought by climate change. But how to balance those risks with the natural desire to become more affluent and enjoy better living standards?

For those looking to escape the poverty trap and settle on a route to higher incomes, the Kuznets curve (see Chapter 3) is likely to remain, especially for those embracing the concrete phase. The question is to what degree that curve can be squashed. It's possible that those in the earlier stages of economic development might, with the right kind of financial assistance and technical know-how, be able to flatten that curve, make it towards economic prosperity while limiting the emissions and climate cost incurred. What role should richer nations play in helping them to do so?

While it is the wealthiest nations who have so far been the biggest contributors to global emissions, it is the poorer ones who are paying the biggest price. Although trillions of dollars will be incurred by the biggest polluters, they are the ones with the deepest pockets, even if their populations may baulk at the cost. Meanwhile the poorer nations will face a bill of hundreds of billions not only to help them towards greener growth but to adapt to the devastation wrought by climate change, much of it the result of others' actions. Who is going to fund such a cost?

In recognition of this, the initiative of climate finance was introduced, encouraging large-scale investments from wealthier nations into projects that will help developing nations adapt to the effects of climate change and reduce their emissions without harming their emergent economies. Developed countries agreed to mobilise $100 billion in climate finance per year by 2020, and subsequently agreed to extend this out to 2025. That was intended to come via public funds (e.g. richer countries' aid agencies or national or regional development banks) or private finance, the idea being that those institutions would be given the confidence to invest on seeing that public funds were prepared to stump up cash. In any case, that $100 billion is a fraction of what will be needed. It was the private funds that proved hardest to mobilise at first, especially when it came to channelling money to the poorest countries, leading to accusations of a half-hearted commitment by richer nations to help their poorer counterparts.

Monitoring how much money has already gone into the scheme often relies on submissions from the donor countries and organisations themselves. That has led to warnings from charities and NGOs that the figures risk being inflated and could include loans that might have happened anyway. However, preliminary data suggests the target was achieved in 2022. Nevertheless, the agreement out of COP 28 acknowledged the 'growing gap' between the needs of developing countries and the money provided. The text stopped short of requiring developed countries to provide more support. But unlocking and encouraging those funds may be key to future success.

There's also the question of where the money is being channelled. The Paris Agreement aimed for a balance between projects aimed at curbing emissions and those that help people adapt to the effects of climate change. But the OECD figures suggest over twice as much went to the former – largely projects in greener energy generation or transport – as the latter. Private finance, in particular, has been entirely geared towards such investment, be it solar plants or electric cars, perhaps unsurprisingly, given the returns they promise. This may be of timely use in helping to decarbonise the development of recipient nations, but such funding struggles to compete with that which is still geared towards high-carbon projects. Moreover, the very poorest nations were more likely to miss out altogether, lacking the expertise and resources to navigate systems to secure funding.

This leaves the ability of developing nations to adapt to climate change – from developing more climate-resilient crops to building flood defences – lagging behind.

However, when it comes to the challenges of building safe and affordable housing and infrastructure, change is happening. 'Avoid-Shift-Improve' has become the mantra when it comes to building the more carbon-friendly infrastructure of the future: avoid building new structures or using new and carbon-intensive materials where possible; shift towards more sustainable materials – biomass or bamboo perhaps; and improve the energy efficiency of the production of the material and processes already typically used.

Nowhere is this more important than the areas that will become the centres of population explosion and growth in the coming decades, and that are playing development catch-up. A UN report in 2023 highlighted some examples of improvements that were already under way, and could provide huge potential and hope for the future.

Ghana has traditionally been the biggest importer of cement in West Africa, as local production was hampered by the lack of suitable limestone, but it has increasingly turned to the use of local low-carbon alternatives, such as clay-based cement, which are manufactured and supplied by local businesses. The UN urges public procurement to wield their purchasing power in this area, and the influence of city planners and developers has been crucial in driving the growth of use of such materials.

Meanwhile, in Senegal, one of the biggest cement companies, Sococim, is using groundnut hulls as a source of alternate fuel, and trialling aquatic weed biomass to construct walls and roofing products. That process has been funded by an injection of funds worth $200 million from the International Financing Corporation, the investment arm of the World Bank, and loans from private banks, the former giving the latter a bit of a nudge – but also the confidence to make the leap. The money will also ultimately help to modernise an existing clinker plant near Dakar, improving fuel efficiency. Not only is the investment a spur to produce revolutionary technology but it also offers solutions for some of the country's housing needs, as well as providing quality jobs.

If projects like these can be replicated at scale, perhaps developing countries can find a way to squash that Kuznets curve after all without compromising development and prosperity.

༄

Unlike so much in this book, there are few ways in which consumers themselves can drive change in this area. That will be dictated by policy-makers, investment flows and builders themselves.

Given that turning steel and concrete green isn't easy, particularly in the short term, and that its use is not going to evaporate, hopes must fall on an acceleration in technology such as CCS that can mitigate its impact economically and efficiently. But this is an area where we're playing catch-up. For now, global producers will have to contend with the costs of integrating greener practices into their industrial processes while risking being undercut by cheaper, dirtier alternatives, unless they can find a way to prop up their industries with public money. Or unless private sources of finance are prepared to take a leap of faith and invest in what could be the lucrative technologies of the future. For there are alternatives being explored and coming to market: hemp-based reinforcements for structures that can be used instead of steel, for example.

It is becoming an increasingly topical issue in many countries. Under President Biden's 'Buy Clean Initiatives', public projects are meant to prioritise the use of low-carbon materials. As the edict points out, the federal government is the biggest direct purchaser in the world; it's the prime example of using that purchasing power to drive change and production at scale.

The new mantra of Avoid-Shift-Improve is also gaining traction around the world. Already, there are burgeoning projects, such as the recycling of cement into other structures, either wholesale or as modular parts, and an increased focus on repurposing buildings. But it needs to go a lot further. Researchers at McKinsey estimate that 2.6 billion tonnes of carbon dioxide could be avoided or mitigated by 2050 by drawing on circular solutions. If the construction industry needs an added incentive, they also reckon it could add up to financial savings of around £100 billion.

To get there, we need more regulatory overhaul and joined-up thinking, especially by policy-makers. Planning hurdles (such as strict rules over the improvement of heritage buildings) might need to be more pragmatic, for example, and, when it comes to recycling of materials, know-how and opportunities need to be shared on a wider scale.

For many planners and builders, there is still too much emphasis on knocking down unattractive and energy-inefficient structures and replacing them with the more sustainable gleaming temples of the future. As well as being generally wasteful, demolition brings its own environmental problems, as the process releases dust, particulate matter and possibly asbestos fibres into the atmosphere. Improving existing buildings would be better, but that still requires a shift in mindset. More forward-thinking projects are now looking at retaining facades, existing cement-heavy foundations or reusing some of the existing structures rather than simply doing away with old and poorly insulated buildings. But that requires some creativity and can be more costly.

For now, the building boom is still ongoing all over the world, and will continue as populations increasingly shift to work and live in urban centres. Finding greener ways to put up all those high-rises must be the priority, but with little the average person can do about it, we're reliant on the industry itself to find those solutions.

11

Sushi for Dinner

Protecting the oceans from overfishing and more

Home at last, and time for dinner. Too tired to cook, you've ordered sushi from your favourite restaurant: convenient, delicious and healthy. One meal at least that's meatless. And it says the ingredients are sustainably sourced, so that's good for the oceans too. Isn't it?

Over 70 per cent of the globe is made up of oceans, and those waters are not just a habitat for marine life but are essential to humanity's existence. They generate oxygen, regulate the climate, are home to potentially millions of species and provide us with an important source of food.

Fishing is a multi-billion-dollar industry, supporting the livelihoods of those living in coastal communities the world over. The waterways yield 200 million tonnes of fish and seafood every year. The average human's consumption of fish has doubled over the last fifty years, now topping 20 kilograms per year. Demand for fish is growing, expected to nearly double by 2050. But this all comes at a hefty price.

Around 90 per cent of fisheries worldwide are fully fished or overfished. More than a third of the world's fish stocks are being caught at 'biologically unsustainable' levels, according to the UN's Food and Agriculture Organization (FAO). In 1971, the figure was more like 10 per cent; the industrialisation of the sector and mass distribution of fish has prompted this dramatic change. That doesn't just threaten the incomes of those who depend on the sea for their living, but also many marine species. The impact tends to be worse in developing countries. Poor management, inefficiencies and overfishing entail a significant economic cost to those involved too: the World Bank reckons the fishing industry is paying over $80 billion more than it should do per year to land the catch.

In 2015, the UN adopted the aim to 'rapidly rebuild sustainable fish stocks' as one of its Sustainable Development Goals. But, with a fifth of the world's fish caught illegally, and agreements on quotas notoriously difficult to reach, it could take decades to restore some stocks to sustainable levels.

When we fly or sail across the ocean, the waters appear endless and unlimited by the laws of the land. But does anyone own them?

Technically, we all do – and don't. Oceans and seas are a 'global commons': shared resources that simultaneously belong to everyone and no one. Overfishing is a textbook example of the tragedy of the commons. That's where resources that are supposed to be open to all are subject to over-exploitation, as individuals simply pursue their own interests without regard for the accumulated impact.

However, countries can claim 'exclusive economic zones' (EEZs) up to 200 nautical miles from their coastlines, and how they manage the marine resources within those areas is up to them. They can issue licences, set catch limits or ban fishing activity, for example. But while they might increasingly be considering marine protection within their zones, policing activity is a challenge.

There are 150 EEZs, accounting for a third of the world's oceans by surface area (less by volume). But what of the rest? Who is responsible for either exploiting them or protecting them? Welcome to the high seas. Since 1994 activity on the seas has been regulated by the United Nations Convention on the Law of the Sea (UNCLOS), which, among other things, set up the idea of the EEZs. But it didn't make any provision for species preservation. For many years, regional fisheries management organisations were the only tool for like-minded nations to cooperate to improve conservation, but such agreements covered only 1 per cent of the high seas, and enforcing them is a perennial issue.

Then, after two decades of talks, the High Seas Treaty was agreed under UNCLOS and signed by UN member states in September 2023. It's a legal framework for creating massive marine protected areas, geared towards a pledge to protect at least 30 per cent of the planet's land and water by 2030. It's a tall order; some estimates suggested only 3 per cent of such resources were protected at the time of signing.

The treaty's been hailed as a breakthrough; only time will tell how successful it will be in protecting those at risk.

In the meantime, most attempts to tackle overfishing take place at a national level. The challenge is getting many different parties with different interests and priorities – politicians, fishermen, consumers, scientists – to work together. That has proved no easy task.

In Britain, for example, over 110,000 tonnes of cod every year typically goes towards sating the British addiction to fish and chips. It became the battered fish of choice out of convenience: cod grow quickly, are easily caught and have a relatively (for fish) long shelf life. In the 1960s their population in the North Sea exploded, making them affordable. But using cod to satisfy our takeaway craving almost led to the devastation of North Atlantic cod stocks by the start of this millennium. The number of fish had plummeted by over 80 per cent in the course of thirty years, with fisheries seeing a corresponding drop in income. North Atlantic cod was on the brink of extinction.

Cue the 'cod recovery plan' in 2005, which sought to restore stocks by limiting fishing days, decommissioning boats, banning catches in areas vital for breeding and putting larger holes in nets to avoid immature cod being sucked in and wasted. It was the result of painstaking negotiations between the EU (of which the UK was then a member) and Norway, with the agreement specifying how the catch would be divided between each country. National politicians were restricted from overruling this agreement. The result was a triumphant comeback for cod: stocks rose fourfold between 2006 and 2017. The coveted tick from the Marine Stewardship Council, indicating sustainability, was once again awarded to some fisheries.

Unfortunately, the problem soon re-emerged as vessels were given freer rein once again. Stocks couldn't recover fast enough to keep up. Fishing boats returned to waters that hadn't been trawled for many years, disrupting those ecosystems once more. Brexit added further complications. British fishermen had been among some of the most vocal supporters of leaving the EU, accusing politicians of the past of being too generous in the fishing rights they had handed over to other countries. The North Atlantic waters became hotly contested, one of the symbols of 'taking back control'.

Lengthy and heated negotiations followed with Norway. Finally, in March 2021, almost five years after the referendum that triggered Brexit, agreement was reached. It included a deal to cut cod catch by 10 per cent that year, although that was a smaller reduction than some scientists would have liked. Being outside the EU means the UK must now negotiate annual limits with third-party countries such as Norway, and British fishing crews have subsequently complained of reduced quotas of whitefish, risking their livelihood.

Quotas are an important tool in making a difference, but they can't be the only one; fishermen depend on big enough catches to survive, and fish forms an important part of our diet. Some species, like cod, are more threatened than others, so one way to make things more sustainable is switching up what's on the menu. In the UK, the MSC has offered consumers guidance on more sustainable alternatives, although their labelling applies to less than half of fish and seafood available. For consumers, judging the provenance of imported fish is far harder.

Hake is one of the widely touted alternatives to cod. In the twenty-first century, hake has gone through the same population boom that cod did in the 1960s. Now plentiful in supply, it is currently one of the most sustainable options and has become a feature on many chip-shop menus. Alternatives need to be considered and managed carefully, lest they too run the risk of being depleted to unsustainable levels. The real challenge, however, has been getting British customers, unaccustomed to hake's taste and texture, to bite. While it's popular on the Continent, and plenty is caught off our shores, only a tiny percentage is consumed here; over 95 per cent is exported. For now, cod is still the preferred choice.

North Atlantic cod has become the most widely cited example both of overfishing and of attempts at fisheries management. It's an example that shows just how tricky the issue can be. Even with agreement, as the EU has found, fish don't respect national boundaries. Such management requires multilateral agreement. It's not just political and economic interests that need to be balanced; politicians also need to defer to scientists.

Once targets have been agreed, there is then the question of how to enforce them. Some countries have resorted to the use of technology to help manage their stocks. Morocco, for example, has invested in a satellite-based Vessel Monitoring System. All fishing boats above a certain size are fitted with tracking beacons, so that they can be monitored in real time to catch those operating within unregulated areas or practising illegally. Fish stocks have been depleting, but half a million Moroccans depend on their existence for their own survival. It's a difficult balancing act between the survival of fishermen and the survival of fishing stock.

In Peru, meanwhile, the government has looked at how those livelihoods can be diverted. The country specialises in anchoveta, a species related to anchovies, but it is not found on plates. Instead, it's a source of omega-3-rich fish oil and fishmeal for livestock and aquaculture around the world, making it vital for food security. In the 1970s, overfishing and ocean-current changes prompted by increasingly frequent weather events meant the stock was at risk of collapse.

How to prevent such a disaster for the Peruvian economy? Little was actively done at first to remedy the situation, but better weather conditions and reduced fishing (largely due to a lack of fish) allowed the species to recover – until the late 1990s, when the same pressures once again took their toll. A quota system was finally introduced in 2009, based on the advice of scientists, with an eye to replenishing stocks to a sustainable level, and a quarter of the anchoveta fleet was retired between 2009 and 2015. Workers who subsequently had to leave the industry were supported through loans provided by the World Bank as well as training and advice to help them to move to other sectors. Quotas were adhered to, and as a result not only did numbers improve, but anchoveta could typically grow to a larger size, fetching a higher price for Peru's catch.

There is no easy solution to overfishing. It requires the global community to come together, but persuading countries to limit the economic benefits gained from fishing is no easy task. FAO figures show that seven countries account for nearly half of capture. China produces 15 per cent of the total, Indonesia and Peru share second place with 7 per cent apiece, with India not far behind. Russia, the USA and Vietnam round out that top seven. As its own waters are depleted, China in particular has been casting its net further afield, including in the lesser-scrutinised waters of some Latin American and African nations.

Given the industry's role in economic and food security, tens of billions of dollars are spent in government subsidies globally to support the estimated 600 million livelihoods that depend at least partially on fisheries and aquaculture, with 59 million involved in primary fish production. As part of the UN's Sustainable Development Goals, it is looking to eliminate fishing subsidies, which it claims encourage overcapacity and overfishing by encouraging catch where it shouldn't be happening. Far from protecting the subsistence farmer, analysts argue these subsidies disproportionately benefit the largest fishers.

The World Trade Organization, the global commerce overseers, thrashed out a 'pivotal agreement' in 2022 after two decades of discussion to curb these harmful subsidies linked to overfished stocks. Getting countries to back it, however, is another matter. Two-thirds of members must accept it. As of October 2023, only 51 out of 164 – less than a third – had done so.

The wheels of international agreements turn slowly. By the time we arrive there, it could be too late.

∽

While overfishing is an urgent environmental issue we need to tackle, it's certainly not the only threat currently posed to our oceans and their inhabitants.

Bycatch is a big deal. 'Dolphin friendly' on a tin of tuna means the fleet didn't intentionally target a feeding pod of dolphins, yet they may have been unintentional casualties. Becoming entangled in fishing gear leads to the deaths of an estimated 300,000 whales and dolphins every year. Figures are hard to come by; no one wants to boast about the unwitting destruction of other sea life in the bid to fill our plates. But the World Wildlife Fund reckons about 40 per cent of fish caught worldwide are unwanted bycatch; they may be returned dead or dying back into the water. It's a massive problem that won't feature on any packaging, but the most forward-looking fishers and governments are trying to address the issue.

Fish farms pose yet more problems. They came about to satisfy our growing appetites for marine creatures and help improve food security, and quickly expanded. The amount produced by fish farms has now overtaken fisheries. But rearing fish in a controlled environment – aquaculture – creates its own hazards if not properly managed. Farming practices such as pesticides or antibiotics can affect nearby species; disease spreads easily among farmed stock and jumps to wild species; fish feed can be high in phosphorous and nitrogen; fish waste can cause oxygen-depleting algae. Managing those risks takes careful regulation and oversight.

The list goes on. Fuel consumption for vessels and fisheries is high. Abandoned fishing gear litters the ocean. Discarded nets, lines and ropes now account for nearly half of the Great Pacific Garbage Patch, according to the World Wildlife Fund. Certain fishing gear and practices, such as bottom trawling (dragging nets along the seabed), can damage marine environments. Bottom trawling is also guilty of a much bigger transgression: carbon is stored in the seabed, and when it gets disturbed and released, it is absorbed into the water. According to one study, the practice might release as much carbon as the aviation industry, with China, Russia, Italy and the UK topping the list of culprits.

This is a problem. The oceans are a vast carbon sink, absorbing about 30 per cent of the carbon dioxide from the atmosphere. Up to ten times more carbon is stored in coastal habitats than in tropical forests. The more excess we've been producing, the more the water has been soaking up, from both above and below. And the ever-increasing level of carbon leads to acidification of the oceans.

Among other problems, acidification exacerbates ocean warming, which is already taking place thanks to the rising temperature of our planet. Researchers found that the top 2-kilometre layer of the oceans' water absorbed fourteen times as much energy over 2021 as in 2020. The increase alone was equal to over a hundred times the energy generated by the entire globe in 2020. And warming in turn leads to deoxygenation.

If none of those things – acidification, warming, deoxygenation – sound good, it's because they aren't. All three take their toll on marine species.

Take coral reefs for one. Corals form skeletons of calcium carbonate, which provide reefs where species can shelter, supporting entire ecosystems. When waters become more acidic, those structures are at risk of dissolving, and they are also vulnerable to rising temperatures. Coral reefs have halved over the space of fifty years, and one study claims they risk becoming unviable by 2050 unless action to protect and regenerate them is taken.

But it's not just creatures under the water that are affected by the changing conditions; they also have a negative impact on us. The more that heat, that energy, builds up in the ocean, the higher the risk of extreme weather events and rising sea levels. It's a ticking time bomb for low-lying communities and habitats. In fact, the devastation is already costing us dear: a report from Christian Aid put the financial losses to the economy from extreme weather in 2021 at over $300 billion, with flooding in Europe costing upwards of $40 billion, damage from Hurricane Ida in North America totalling $65 billion, and flooding and typhoons in Asia costing $24 billion. In 2022 the figure was slightly lower at $280 billion, though the data is thought to be incomplete.

Clearly action must be taken to protect the oceans, to preserve biodiversity, to maintain a valuable resource, and to limit the effects of devastating weather on human settlements.

The oceans themselves could help to provide part of the solution to defuse the crisis. Enter blue carbon, literally underwater. Animals and plants living in or around the oceans make a key contribution to absorbing the naturally occurring carbon on the planet. Mangroves, for example, like other coastal wetlands, suck up carbon dioxide from the air to store in their roots and branches. When they die, the carbon can be stored in the soil and sediment for thousands of years.

The 'big three' stores – mangroves, salt marshes and seagrass – account for more than half of blue carbon contained in sediment; over 200 million tonnes of carbon dioxide might be captured annually. But if these areas are damaged or degrade, all that carbon starts to be released, which means these areas are in urgent need of conservation. As awareness of the potential problem grows, there have been calls for accounting systems for blue carbon, to log and evaluate marine and coastal ecosystems, so that they can be protected.

While mangrove restoration could be viable, large-scale seagrass restoration is more challenging. It is shrinking by 7 per cent per year and replanting is painstaking and labour-intensive work. But it can reap rewards; as a carbon sink, coastal wet-lands can be over thirty times as effective as rainforests. So there is a considerable potential prize at stake: one report suggests full restoration of the Big Three could absorb the equivalent of 3 per cent of the world's greenhouse gases, so it would be worth our while to pursue such a project, both to help tackle the problem of climate change and to preserve a resource that is so important to our daily lives and the biodiversity of our planet.

With energy companies and investors chasing the next big thing, there are mangrove restoration projects in Kenya, Vietnam and – the biggest of all – in the Arabian Sea off Pakistan. The World Bank and some governments are putting in grants to explore the potential of blue carbon, but as yet the data on its viability and return are very sparse.

Such projects could also help nations to meet their goals for net zero. Commitments made to keep these mangrove forests intact can be purchased and traded on the global market to compensate for carbon emissions made elsewhere. Known as carbon offsets, essentially consumers and companies pay to use a polluting project, and those funds go to projects that absorb carbon: planting more trees, for example, or preventing them from being cut down. The schemes are not without controversy, though; one investigation threw doubt on their effectiveness. But they are a tool that is attractive to companies looking to go about business as usual or expand without increasing their climate guilt.

Where do we go from here? The preservation of our oceans is a vast problem, requiring vast solutions. A lot will depend on the adoption and successful implementation of international agreements. The breakthroughs with the High Seas Treaty and the WTO's work on fishing subsidies bring new hope after many years and are not to be scoffed at. But, without international cooperation, more concerted government oversight and policing of the fishing industry, they will amount to little. More pressure from consumers might be needed to keep the industry on track as well.

The oceans are at the mercy of our actions, but we must recognise that we are at their mercy too. Preserving the delicate marine ecosystems are crucial to the health of our planet, to our way of life, perhaps even to the very survival of our species. The oceans will be judge and jury on how we choose to proceed. The sentence they deliver will be served by us all.

12

The Weekly Shop

Ending our reliance on palm oil

As the day draws to an end, another of our modern conveniences appears: the arrival of the supermarket shop. Your weekly trawl through the aisles replaced by a one-stop drop, covering everything from food to cleaning products, even cosmetics. But what you don't know is that many of this vast and diverse range of products have one ingredient in common: palm oil. And it's doing a whole lot of damage.

Palm oil is a seemingly magic ingredient; it has such a multitude of uses that it typically appears in half the products on our supermarket shelves, from deodorants to pizza, noodles to margarine. It makes your lipstick glide on, your shampoo lather up and leaves your hair squeaky clean, as well as making your chocolate melt smoothly and your cookies vegan-friendly. It enables cleaning products to foam, blends with other oils, acts as a natural preservative (as it evades oxidation), prevents ice cream from melting, and can withstand high temperatures for frying. It's an exceptionally versatile vegetable oil. So versatile, in fact, that it is almost impossible to pinpoint its presence in our products. It's everywhere, but it turns up in ingredients lists under a hugely confusing variety of names, so it's easy to escape notice even if you're looking for it.

Vegetable oil, vegetable fat, palm kernel, palm kernel oil, palm fruit oil, sodium palmate, palmitate, palm olein, glyceryl stearate, stearic acid, elaeis guineensis, palmitic acid, palm stearin, palmitoyl oxostearamide, palmitoyl tetrapeptide-3, sodium laureth sulphate, sodium lauryl sulphate, sodium kernelate, sodium palm kernelate, sodium lauryl lactylate/sulphate, hydrogenated palm glycerides, ethyl palmitate, octyl palmitate, palmityl alcohol . . . all of these are basically palm oil or based on the derivatives of the oil.

Some of them – sodium laureth sulphate, for example – can also be made from coconut or petroleum oil. But the label might not disclose that. In the absence of a chemistry degree, avoiding products that use palm oil is virtually impossible.

And why would we want to? It's not just miraculous; it's also cheap. It's derived from the fruit of the oil palm tree, which grows in tropical climates. Its low cost reflects the tree's ultra-efficiency as a crop: it yields up to ten times more oil per acre than any other edible vegetable oil.

All of this – and more – has helped palm oil to world domination. When US producers were ordered by law in 2015 to remove artery-clogging trans-fats from their foods – from cakes to crisps – they turned to palm oil. The Bank of England was urged to use a derivative of the oil instead of beef tallow when it started to issue plastic banknotes to make them vegan-friendly.

Pressured to churn out products cheaply amid the cut-throat pressure of globalisation? Hello, palm oil. And when an increasingly affluent population wants to emulate the lifestyle and diet of its richer counterparts, palm oil is the affordable shortcut. Almost half the world's output is consumed in Asia. It's even proved a soothing balm in a time of war. Ukraine is a key source of sunflower seeds used for oil. When its exports paused after the Russian invasion and the cost of sunflower oil soared, it was palm oil that food manufacturers turned to as a still affordable and versatile substitute.

The use of palm oil can be traced back centuries, but only in the last fifty years or so has it grown to become an intrinsic part of our lives. Some 70 million tonnes of palm oil are now produced every year, and demand is set to triple within the next thirty years. The impact of this ubiquitous enabler on every part of our consumption has been seismic.

Its impact on the planet has also been seismic, but in a completely different sense.

The oil palm tree originated in West Africa. Its first notable role in history was a dark one: it was used as a staple foodstuff to sustain slaves on ships that plied the transatlantic routes, and was also rubbed into their skins to give them a healthier appearance ahead of auction. Following the abolition of slavery in Britain, palm oil found a new customer base. Used as an alternative to tallow in soap and candles, it gained fans such as Lord William Lever, founding father of the company that would become Unilever. Towards the end of the nineteenth century, palm oil was also being used as a key ingredient in an innovative cheap alternative to butter: margarine.

But West African communities were reluctant to spare the land to cater to booming Western demand, preferring to supply through their own smallholdings, which led to producers resorting to forced labour and colonial-government coercion. Eventually though, potential customers turned their sights elsewhere.

The oil palm had been introduced to South-East Asia in the 1870s as an ornamental shrub. Belgian botanist Adrien Hallet noted that such trees appeared to thrive better in these hot and humid lands – with fairly constant tropical temperatures, evenly distributed rainfall and reliable sunshine – than in their native soils. He set up the first commercial palm plantation in Sumatra in 1911. Spurred on by palm oil's use as a machine lubricant, other Dutch colonisers went about setting up large-scale plantations there and in Borneo, partly to shift people away from the densely populated area of Java to areas where food supplies were more plentiful, and, in doing so, availed themselves of a source of cheap labour. Hallet also supplied the seedlings for plantations subsequently set up in Malaysia. Drawing on unfettered access to land and teams of low-paid migrant workers, producers were able to cater to exploding demand.

Palm oil became an established route out of poverty for these nations, and a way of integrating into the global economy. Malaysia was already a significant exporter of palm oil by the time it gained independence in 1957, with the guaranteed custom of Britain's Ministry of Food. As pollination techniques improved, the cultivation of oil palms was seen as an increasingly attractive export from the 1960s onwards, particularly when the price of Malaysia's other main crop – rubber – was falling on international markets, as new synthetic alternatives emerged in the age of plastics.

Meanwhile, in Indonesia, the industry had been struggling in the aftermath of the Second World War, but it was revived in the 1970s with help from the likes of the World Bank, which supported the push for smaller farmers to take on more palm cultivation. Later, growing exports of natural resources was a plank of the IMF's rescue package in the aftermath of the Asian financial crisis of the late 1990s, which had decimated manufacturing production.

Some 90 per cent of the world's palm oil is now produced in Indonesia and Malaysia. It is the biggest export for Indonesia, the largest economy in South-East Asia, and it accounts for $1 in every $7 of income in Malaysia. Both through direct employment and linked industries, palm oil provides livelihoods for millions in those two countries alone (although jobs on plantations themselves can be not only highly skilled but dangerous).

There are hundreds of palm-oil mills in Malaysia and Indonesia, with carefully arrayed production lines of industrial machines that appear a world away from the sweeping plantations they service. Each will draw fruit from many suppliers and stand ready to receive it within hours of harvest. The bunches of palm fruit are sterilised by steaming, then the fruit is stripped from the branches and shaped into cakes, which are pressed to release the oil.

Despite the many churning mills, it's the vast plantations of oil palm trees that are the key problem. Or, rather, the vast swathes of rainforests that are being cleared to make way for them: charity Rainforest Rescue claims that the equivalent of

300 football fields of forest is cleared and burned every hour in Indonesia. These are some of the world's most biodiverse lands that are being destroyed: habitats for already endangered species, such as orangutans and Sumatran elephants.

The loss of forests is an issue because they help balance carbon in the atmosphere by producing oxygen and sucking up carbon dioxide. The situation is made worse as the burning releases more greenhouse gases into the air. What's more, many of these forests are on carbon-rich peat soils, and when they are disrupted yet more carbon dioxide is chugged into the air at an alarming rate. So much so that Indonesia bears the burden of at times being the third-biggest contributor of greenhouse gases after China and the USA, despite its economy being a twentieth of the size of the latter's.

Indonesia has unveiled ambitions to see its greenhouse gas emissions peak in 2030 and aim for net zero emissions by 2060. That relies heavily on reduced deforestation and increased reforestation – effectively returning forests to a net-carbon sink by 2030. Malaysia has also pledged to halt deforestation by 2030, but previous attempts have failed. It has also said it won't compromise on its growth ambitions. Moreover, its energy will still come primarily from coal.

The environmental Kuznets curve (see Chapter 3) – whereby economic development initially leads to more environmental degradation before it's reduced – may still be alive in these nations. The ambition to keep a nation prospering is at odds with the aims of halting deforestation.

What can be done? One option would be to reduce demand. As realisation has hit about the ecological and environmental cost of palm oil, more climate-conscious consumers have taken to studying ingredient labels, in an effort to cut the offending substance out of their diets and bathroom cabinets. Good luck with that – as we've seen, it's a difficult task, the labels a minefield to navigate.

But, perhaps surprisingly, many conservationists argue that phasing out palm oil isn't the best solution. Given that it is such a high-yielding crop, swapping it for other oils – sunflower, rapeseed or soybean, for example – would require a far larger quantity of land, as they're much less efficient crops. That could disrupt other ecosystems, destroying habitats for wildlife and plants on a wider scale. Plus there's the multitude of livelihoods, in particular smallholder farmers, that could be affected.

What could be more beneficial is to ensure palm oil is produced responsibly without excessively damaging ecosystems or contributing to climate change. And that can be done.

In 2004, the World Wildlife Fund, on the back of growing public awareness and outrage, pushed growers, manufacturers and retailers to establish the Roundtable on Sustainable Palm Oil (RSPO). What criteria have to be met to wear this badge? According to RSPO: 'No primary forests or areas which contain significant concentrations of biodiversity or fragile ecosystems, or areas which are fundamental to meeting basic or traditional cultural needs of local communities, can be cleared.' It also requires a significant reduction in deployment of pesticides and fires, and that workers are treated in accordance with local and international labour standards. Communities should be 'informed and consulted' before the development of new plantations in their vicinity. And certification is determined by independent auditors. RSPO members can opt to produce or use only sustainable palm oil (known as segregated palm oil as it's kept physically separate from conventionally produced palm oil and is traced through the supply chain) and many increasingly do – but actually they don't have to. They can instead buy certificates equal to the amount of palm oil they use, even though that certified palm oil might not end up in their products.

Since RSPO's inception, the amount of certified output has grown rapidly. Within a decade, a fifth of the world's palm oil was certified as sustainable, but it's yet to become the norm in the industry. Meanwhile, some 75 per cent of the remaining wild orangutans in Borneo live in areas that are still not officially protected.

Where activists and pressure groups have raised awareness, businesses are increasingly following, with many looking to cut their use of palm oil, but data is still playing catch-up. As is the system itself. Customers wanting to check if their shopping basket contains sustainable palm oil can look up the contents on RSPO's lists or turn to the scorecard produced by the World Wildlife Fund. But it's very difficult for anyone – consumers, suppliers, regulators – to keep an eye on what's what. The myriad names that palm oil and its derivatives go under are a clue to just how intricate the supply chains can be. But also, in most instances, traceability starts at the mill; it doesn't go back to the field. The complexity of the system in which it is grown and sold makes it very difficult for businesses to have complete control of their sources – even if they want to. The system was set up to ensure the complex chains of globalisation could be fed swiftly and cheaply in bulk, not with an eye to accountability and transparency. It has evolved more by accident than design; it's not easy to unravel.

Even Nestlé, which typically ranks highly on the WWF scorecard, fell short of an aim to have 100 per cent of its palm oil classed deforestation-free by 2020, although it managed to score 95.6 per cent in 2022. It claimed it can trace over 95 per cent of palm oil back to the mill of origin and two-thirds to the plantation level. In a multitude of goods – from pet food to confectionery – the food giant used almost half a million tonnes of palm oil in 2021 for goods sold all over the world.

And there is further work afoot here; technology is increasingly being used to ensure that each bunch of fruit can be tracked back not just to a farmer but an individual field, to cut deforestation out of the chain. Multinationals such as Unilever, Mars and Nestlé have invested in new satellite technologies and joined up to monitor deforestation in the vicinity of the mills that supply them. A group of palm-oil producers and buyers is developing a new, publicly available radar-based system for monitoring forests.

Despite these efforts, critics such as Greenpeace are still concerned that the certification doesn't go far enough, that standards are too weak and that companies may be neither audited nor penalised adequately. And not all oil has to be derived from fully certified sources for a product to be marked sustainable. At worst, the scheme might serve as a greenwashing shield for those who are essentially pursuing business as usual.

Given these concerns, RSPO too is a work in progress, and the rules are evolving. The latest iteration has adopted a total ban on deforestation, and stronger provisions for protecting high-carbon-stock forests, peat soils and rights of plantation workers, in line with pressure not just from activists but from consumers and investors too.

The people behind RSPO hoped that keeping the rules relatively loose would make the scheme accessible and more viable for producers to sign up to. But, by its own admission, it also means many producers don't bother to aim for the highest level of certification. The cost and complexity of doing so doesn't guarantee a correspondingly higher return if their customers won't bite. Those signing up have to be confident that there is the market out there for a sustainable product: buyers who are willing to pay the premium. Less aware or less affluent customers may not do so, particularly in core markets such as India. Elsewhere, supermarket profit margins tend to be very thin, typically around 5 per cent, the market for grocery items is very competitive, and customers are price sensitive, meaning the market for non-sustainable sources looks pretty much guaranteed, for now.

Thousands of businesses and the products they make depend on palm oil. Without an alternative that can compete on price, quality and versatility, it isn't going anywhere. It's a key part of our everyday lives in billions of small ways, and it's not easy to replace. It is unlikely that our toothpaste, cakes and noodles are going to be palm-oil-free any time soon.

It's the economics of supply and demand, and the system in which the oil is produced and sold, that underpin this issue. For the governments of Malaysia and Indonesia, and the palm-oil growers, it's the land – the oil produced on it, and the billions of products then sold around the world every day – that brings wealth; it's not the biodiverse forests and peat-rich soils that are being cleared and burned.

But there is a shift taking place around the world that recognises those forests are a form of wealth in and of themselves and worth protecting not just as an environmental cause but for the benefit of the country. It's a major change that is worth discussing because it's going to drive a lot of the developments taking place in the coming years.

For some time now, conservation – protecting the natural habitats of the world's animals and plants and ensuring their survival, combating either deliberate or unwitting actions – has often been seen as out of kilter with a push for prosperity: a 'nice to have' rather than a 'do or fail'.

However, in 2020, a study from the World Economic Forum and global accounting firm PwC found that half of the world economy, representing about $44 trillion, is dependent on the natural world and high-functioning biodiversity. Construction, agriculture (including those vast palm-oil plantations), and food and beverages are the industries that are the most reliant because they either draw directly on resources such as forests and oceans or they depend on clean water, healthier soils and the weather. Then there are other industries – aviation, travel, chemicals and pharmaceuticals, for example – that have what the WEF called 'hidden' dependencies on the natural world, as they provide vital components for their supply chains that might not be immediately apparent. They too are at risk of costly disruption. Around two-thirds of cancer drugs, for example, are based on natural products or synthetic products inspired by nature.

A separate report from insurance giant Swiss Re also flagged that one in five countries will see ecosystems buckle in the coming decades due to the devastation of the natural world. That spells significant disruption for the very industries (and their customers) that feed off them. Put simply: many large businesses and economies will fail without a functioning natural world.

The WEF report concluded that it's the richest economies – the USA, China and the EU – that stand to lose the most in total cash terms as their industries are the largest and most valuable. The ones with the deepest pockets are at most financial risk, so they should have the greatest self-interest to act. As the ones with the greatest power and influence, they are also best placed to assume leadership in this global issue. However, many still need to be convinced it is in their interests first.

In 2021, the UN claimed the world would need to quadruple its annual investment in nature to avoid a climate and biodiversity crisis by 2050. Avoiding the breakdown of natural ecosystem 'services' such as clean water, food and flood protection would require just 0.1 per cent of global GDP every year towards restoring agriculture, managing pollution and conserving land. The payback could be enormous, the consequences of neglect catastrophic.

The UN report advised policy-makers to divert funds from detrimental agricultural and fossil fuel subsidies towards protecting nature. As part of that, governments need to start weaving the financial value of nature into their decision-making and growth-planning.

How do we bring ecosystems and biodiversity into the growth equation? How do we make those forests in Indonesia and Malaysia stack up against the straightforward, more obvious financial benefits?

An increasing number of economists believe it's time to tear down the old growth models, instead advocating a form of accounting that incorporates our 'natural capital assets'.

GDP, or Gross Domestic Product, is the common economic scorecard around the world used to measure the income, output or expenditure (in theory, the three should be the same) of a nation for every quarter of every year. It's a quick way to measure prosperity, using easily accessible and quantifiable data. It's become the shorthand for our standard of living.

GDP was first devised as a measure in the seventeenth century, refined as a modern concept by Simon Kuznets (yes, him of the curve) in the 1930s, and then adopted as the yardstick of financial success in 1944 at the Bretton Woods Conference, where the modern international financial system was established. It thus became entrenched in policy-makers' goals for the duration of the twentieth century, and into the twenty-first.

When it comes to GDP, bigger is always better. The higher the number, the richer the country. But Kuznets himself warned of its limitations: GDP is not a measure of overall economic welfare – certainly not of individual welfare – and it is by no means comprehensive. He said, 'Distinctions must be kept in mind between quantity and quality of growth, between costs and returns, and between the short and long run. Goals for more growth should specify more growth of what and for what.'

His words have resonated with many critics of GDP: pump oil into the sea, or allow a nuclear plant to leak, and GDP turns a blind eye to the destruction. It does, however, notch up the money spent on the clean-up operations, and the cost of any increase in healthcare needed, as an increase in GDP – in other words, a win. As we've seen, Indonesia is the biggest economy in South-East Asia – it has the biggest GDP, something to be proud of. But if we were to take into account the harm one of its biggest industries is doing to its natural assets, would it look like such a success story?

In 2021, a high-profile review conducted by the University of Cambridge's Professor Sir Partha Dasgupta echoed these sentiments. What was groundbreaking was that this was not an academic paper but a review conducted on behalf of the British government. The report concluded that much of our modern use of GDP is based on a faulty application of economics. It doesn't measure our accumulated stock of wealth and does not include the depletion of natural assets.

Dasgupta showed that between 1992 and 2014, when looking at the usual measures of wealth, the world appeared to have become much richer. But during that time, the stock of natural capital per person declined by nearly 40 per cent. In short, we've been measuring success – what it looks like and what it takes – wrong. Only a rapid overhaul of how society measures economic success will stem the rapid decline of biodiversity that threatens civilisation as we know it.

One recommendation from the Dasgupta Review was to help slow that decline by devising a better form of national accounting to include natural resources. In short, Dasgupta states that our 'natural capital' (e.g. rainforests or oceans) should be allocated a value, and their degradation or regeneration be measured as our return on that asset – a bit like any other investment portfolio. Ultimately, the review wants us all to recognise that we are 'asset managers' who have an intrinsic self-interest and responsibility for looking out for nature.

So how might we start to think about measuring biodiversity's value? There's the potential loss of human life as a result of collapsing ecosystems. That's a big cost. As we've seen, there are goods and services that depend on nature (which helps companies put a monetary value on nature in their accounts). Another is its direct contribution to human health – there are numerous studies that have proved the physical and mental benefits humans derive from nature. We can also count the sheer enjoyment of biodiversity, thinking of nature as an amenity. And there's what's called the 'existence value': even if you never get to see an orangutan in the wild, you might draw comfort from knowing they are safeguarded. They're valuable for their own sake.

The problem is putting an actual monetary value on these things isn't easy. While a fishery might be easy to quantify, the impact of having a healthy ecosystem that allows for, say, pollination, is less so.

Nevertheless, some countries have already started trying to do this. China has experimented with Gross Ecosystem Product, developed by Professor Stephen Polasky at the University of Minnesota, which aims to incorporate aspects of nature into financial measures and decision-making – whether that's the approval of new projects or evaluating if a method of economic growth has been to the detriment of the environment. Polasky's team has been trialling the approach in Qinghai in western China, which is the source of three of the country's major rivers – very valuable natural assets.

The team claims that GEP outpaced GDP in 2000 but only managed 75 per cent of GDP in 2015; it hadn't kept track with its conventional counterpart. But, over those fifteen years, GEP was up 127 per cent, reflecting efforts put into restoration; in that sense it is a useful signpost and analytical tool for measuring progress in sustainable growth. GEP itself is just a number – its real use will be in directing resources via policy-making – for example, in encouraging those with higher GDP who are the beneficiaries of an exploited resource to compensate those disadvantaged by its exploitation. However, if not officially embraced more widely, it will not be an effective factor in policy-making.

In 2011, New Zealand started developing its Living Standards Framework: a dashboard of progress on elements that contribute to New Zealanders' well-being. Drawing on dozens of indicators, it looked broadly at three main categories: 'our people' (the well-being of individuals and communities); 'our country' (the government and organisations responsible for ensuring well-being and prosperity); and 'overall wealth' (including non-standard measures of wealth such as natural capital). However, while its ambitions were lauded by the OECD, that group highlighted the gaps in data available, particularly when it came to natural resources. Unlike the old standby of GDP, it didn't merit much of a mention in New Zealand's 2021 Budget.

It's fair to say that such measures are still in the early stages. If adopted more widely, they could give a very different picture of economic progress in countries such as Indonesia and Malaysia, contradicting their often impressive conventional growth record.

In the meantime, though, GDP remains the yardstick of economic progress, even if its flaws and exclusions are increasingly recognised. The Dasgupta Report recommends policy-makers intervene by regulation and taxes. But many national governments are still trying to increase their GDP by any means necessary. Even if we could reliably place a value on natural resources, they still might not be the priority when stacked up against potential vast short-term profits.

There are those who caution against putting a price on our natural capital at all, for fear that, by placing a monetary value on it, we render biodiversity more likely to be a potential casualty in any cost-benefit analysis for projects. The campaigner George Monbiot argues that positioning nature as another asset to be managed 'is the mindset that has trashed the living world'.

That's why the Dasgupta Report also calls for protections for high-value areas and new global institutions to protect global natural assets – forests, seas and the like. Poorer countries should be subsidised to protect ecosystems, enabling them to ease compromises on development. This might help countries such as Indonesia and Malaysia to balance the immediate financial losses they would incur from preserving, rather than clearing, those forests.

Some estimates suggest that we'll need the equivalent resources of three Earths by 2050 if we are to maintain today's living standards. Technology and more efficient production methods are making steps towards curbing our use of Earth's resources and limiting biodiversity loss. But we need to go further to overhaul the way we consume and produce if we're really going to protect our natural capital. We need to shake the exploitative attitude that humans have adopted for so long. We need to review the accepted wisdom of the economic systems that prioritise tangible profits over every single other factor. Without such fundamental changes, effective measures to protect these essential resources will never take hold. And we need it to happen fast, because not only is it cheaper to conserve than to restore degraded resources, there will come a point where it's too late to reverse the damage.

When it comes to palm oil, profit clearly still comes first. Add to that its sheer omnipresence, the difficulty in deciphering ingredient lists and the complexity in the supply chains, and we will probably find it in our shopping baskets for years to come. For now, your simple daily rituals such as squeezing a tube of toothpaste or grabbing a slice of cake continue to play a part in one of the most rapidly evolving and important stories of our time.

Acknowledgements

Writing so many thousands of words in a rapidly evolving field brings many challenges – to overcome those means leaning on the advice, support and insights of others; I am grateful to them all.

It's been a gift to work with the brilliant editing duo Pippa Crane and Jennie Condell once again. This is the second time I've disregarded the advice that while everyone has a book inside them, that's where it should, in most cases, stay. Thank you to them for their endless patience, energy and creativity as they've refined and shaped my ideas for the page. And to publicists Amy Greaves and Emma Finnigan for their sterling work.

To my indefatigable agent and friend Mary Greenham for embarking on another project with good humour, sage advice and lashings of gossip.

I am indebted to the many analysts, business leaders, policy-makers and action groups who have been generous with their insights.

I'm privileged to have a day job that allows me to cover some of the tumultuous economic developments of the modern age. But it's also one that shares characteristics with a toddler; engaging but vociferous in its demands, even in anti-social hours. So above all, I'm grateful to my family – my husband, children and parents for their support and tolerance as I added another job to the constant juggling – and their endurance when the odd plate is dropped. Thank you.

A Note on Sources

This is a fast-moving topic that is constantly evolving, but here are some resources that I have found useful for up-to-date information and statistics relating to the green economy:

Deloitte, https://www2.deloitte.com/uk/en/explore/home.html
Boston Consulting Group, https://www.bcg.com
Ellen MacArthur Foundation, https://www.ellenmacarthur
    foundation.org
Environmental Audit Committee, UK House of Commons,
    https://committees.parliament.uk/committee/62/
    environmental-audit-committee/publications/
Fashion Revolution, https://www.fashionrevolution.org
Food and Agriculture Organization of the United Nations
    (FAO), https://www.fao.org/home/en
Intergovernmental Panel on Climate Change (IPPC),
    https://www.ipcc.ch
International Energy Agency (IEA), https://www.iea.org
McKinsey & Company, https://www.mckinsey.com
Morningstar, https://www.morningstar.co.uk/uk/
Organisation for Economic Co-operation and Development
    (OECD), https://www.oecd.org/unitedkingdom/

Our World in Data, https://ourworldindata.org
The World Bank, https://www.worldbank.org/en/home

For those who wish to explore further some of the issues surrounding the green economy, I highly recommend the following:

Mike Berners-Lee, *How Bad Are Bananas? The Carbon Footprint of Everything* (Profile Books, 2020)

Mark Carney, *Value(s): Building a Better World for All* (William Collins, 2021)

P. Dasgupta, 'The Economics of Biodiversity: the Dasgupta Review' (HM Treasury, February 2021); https://assets. publishing.service.gov.uk/media/602e92b2e90e07660 f807b47/The_Economics_of_Biodiversity_The_Dasgupta_ Review_Full_Report.pdf

Tim Harford, *The Undercover Economist* (Abacus, 2007)

Paul Polman and Andrew Winston, *Net Positive: How Courageous Companies Thrive by Giving More Than They Take* (Harvard Business Review Press, 2021)

Kate Raworth, *Doughnut Economics: Seven Ways to Think Like a 21st-Century Economist* (Random House Business, 2018)

Index

A

access economy 111
acid rain 4
acidification of oceans 224
Advertising Standards
    Authority 144
agriculture 155–6, 165–71
air pollution 5, 71
    ammonia 77, 166–8,
        169–70
    China 58, 61–2, 203–4
    diesel cars 92–3
    Paris 166–8
Airbus 84
al-Shabaab 132
alternative fuels
    aviation industry 83–4
    car industry 94–6
    shipping trade 76–9
aluminium cans 127–8
Amazon (company) 69, 85
Amazon rainforest 158
Amendi 47
ammonia 77, 166–8,
    169–70
aquaculture 223
ArcelorMittal 201
ASOS 41
ATMs 184
Attenborough, Sir David
    116
Audi 96
Australia 57, 98, 99, 184,
    200
aviation industry 81–4
'Avoid-Shift-Improve' 210,
    212

B

Bangladesh: textile industry
    30, 50
Bank of England 185
    central-bank digital
        currency 192–3
    divests from fossil fuel
        investments 141
    polymer banknotes 184,
        230
Baotou, China 58
batteries
    electric vehicles 97–8,
        99–100, 103
    phones 55–6
    recycling 99–100
beef production 158–9
Beijing: smog 61–2
Belt and Road Initiative
    (China) 202–3, 206–7
Benz, Carl 90
Berkshire Hathaway 137
Bessemer, Henry 199
Better Cotton Initiative 31,
    46
Beyond Meat 162–3
Biden, President x, 15, 62,
    125–6
    and aviation industry 84
    'Buy Clean Initiatives'
        212
    and rare earth metal
        supplies 59–60
Bio-bean 180
biodiversity and economics
    239–40
    China 243

natural capital assets
    242–3
    New Zealand 244
biofuels
    aviation industry 83
    car industry 94
    from coffee grounds 180–1
    shipping trade 77
biogas 181–2
biomass 16, 77, 210, 211
bioplastics 129–30
bitcoin 184, 188–94
Bitgreen 193
BlackRock 138. see also
    Fancy, Tariq
blue carbon 225–6
blue hydrogen 78–9
Blue Planet II 116, 131–3
BMW: ev batteries 99
Bolivia: lithium production
    55
bottom trawling 223
BP 6, 18
    Deepwater Horizon
        disaster 75
    and shipping fuel 80
Brazil xi, 6, 98, 186
    meat production 157–8
Break Free From Plastic 119
Brexit 219
Briganti, Chelsea 131
British Airways 83
Buffett, Warren 136–7
'build back better' 151
building industry 195–6
    alternative approaches
        212–13

building industry (contd.)
  carbon capture and
    storage (CCS) 198–9
  carbon footprint 197–8,
    199–200
  cement 197–8, 202,
    210–11
  China 201–7
  concrete 207–8, 210–11
  demolition problems 213
  Japan 205
  steel 199–201, 202–4,
    211–13
  sustainability initiatives
    197–201, 210–11
Burberry 40, 48
Burger King 162
buses 108, 109
businesses and climate
  change 136–8, 144–5
'Buy Clean Initiatives' 212

C

cans, aluminium 127–8
car industry 91–4
  alternative fuels 94–6
  government policies 92,
    102–4, 112–13
  India 104–8
  supply chain & raw
    materials 96–102
carbon border adjustment
  mechanism (CBAM)
  170
carbon capture and storage
  (CCS) 18, 78, 198–9,
  212, 225–6
carbon dioxide. see
  greenhouse gas
  emissions; net zero
  target
Carbon Disclosure Project
  47
carbon footprint. see
  greenhouse gas
  emissions
carbon labelling 160–1
carbon offsetting 82–3,
  225–6
carbon pricing 154, 169–70
carbon sinks 224, 225–6
carbon taxes 24, 154, 201

carbon trading 82–3, 225–6
card payments 183–7
cargo ships: environmental
  impact 70–2
cars 96
  alternatives to 108–12
  diesel 92–3
  electric 71–2, 84, 90,
    93–6
  hybrid 94–5
  petrol 74, 89
  SUVs 91
cash. see money
CBDC (central-bank digital
  currency) 192–3
cement 197–8, 202, 210–11
cheques 186
Chernobyl 9
chicken & poultry 161
child labour 56
Chile: lithium production
  55, 98
China
  air pollution 58, 61–2,
    203–4
  Belt and Road Initiative
    202–3, 206–7
  bitcoin mining 189
  building industry 201–7
  carbon neutral vs energy
    security 65–6
  cement production 202
  coal powered energy 61–2
  cotton production 46
  cycling policies 110
  electric vehicles 96
  fishing industry 221
  food industry 172–3
  government spending on
    renewables 11
  greenhouse gas emissions
    61–2, 63–4
  Gross Ecosystem Product
    243–4
  imported waste 122–3,
    124
  industrialisation 61–2,
    63–4
  investment in green
    technology 65–6
  methane emissions 63
  natural capital assets
    243–4

net zero target 65
overseas building
  development 206–7
phasing out fossil fuels 63
phone manufacture 61
production of hardware
  for renewables 13
rare earth metals 57–9, 61
textile industry 30
trade war with USA
  59–60, 203
circular economy x, 38–40,
  50–1, 97, 212–13
climate change vii–xii, ix,
  5, 174
climate finance initiative
  208–9
climate focused funds 140
clinker 197, 198
Clinton Global Initiative
  131
clothing. see also textile
  industry
  cheap fast fashion 34–6
  designer fashion 37, 40
  effects of washing 35
  luxury brands 37, 40
  recycling 38–9
  renting 38–9
  reselling 38–9
  returns problem 40–1
  returns to landfill problem
    35–6
  virtual fittings 40–1
  waste to landfill problem
    35–6, 48
coal
  China 61–2
  decommissioning 24–5
  greenhouse gas emissions
    4
  phasing out use of 63
  as a stranded asset 18
  United Kingdom 3–4
cobalt batteries 56–7, 98,
  99
Coca-Cola 119, 120, 121,
  126–7, 129
cod 218–19
coffee grounds, fuel from
  179–80
coffee production 175–7
commodities market 72–3

commodities supercycles
72–3
concrete 196–7, 207–8,
210–13
construction industry. *see*
building industry
consumer choice 2–3, 21–3,
37, 47, 160
consumer habits x–xi, 245
aviation 82
car industry 93
clothing 51
energy 21–3
fishing industry 219–20
food industry 160
palm oil 234–5
phones 67–8
consumer trust 93, 150
consumers
demand for fast fashion
34–5
household energy use
2–3
impact of green issues on
ix–x
influence of x–xi, 43–5
micro-investing apps 137
pension funds 148–50
pressures on to buy more
36
price sensitivity of 37
cooking oils as fuel 83
COP 26 (Glasgow) 62–3,
139
COP 28 (Dubai) viii, x–xi,
209
coral reefs 224
cost-of-living crisis xii, 24,
162–3, 171
cotton
forced labour 46
organic 32, 46
production 28–9, 31, 46
recycling 33
Covid-19 pandemic
effects on oil prices 73
impact of xi, 59
and single use plastic 134
cows 158–9
cryptocurrencies 184,
188–94
Curtis, Richard 149
cycling 109–10

D
dairy production
decline in consumption
163–5
greenhouse gas emissions
157, 158–60
Dasgupta Report 242, 244,
245
Deepwater Horizon disaster
75
deforestation 234
Democratic Republic of the
Congo (DRC) 56, 98
Denmark 10–11, 19–21, 25
deoxygenation of oceans
224
Depop 39
designer fashion 37, 40
developing countries
adapt to climate change
210
Chinese building projects
in 206–7
climate finance initiative
208–9
growth vs environmental
degradation 208
overfishing 216
plastic waste exported to
122–4
plastic waste produced
by 118
textile industry 29–30,
46–7
victims of climate change
208–10
diesel cars 92–3
digital currency 184,
188–94
disposable lifestyle 115
Dogecoin 191
DONG (Danish Oil and
Natural Gas) 19–20
dyes 29

E
eBay 39
economics
and climate change
vii–xii, ix
commodities supercycles
72–3

GDP as a measure of
prosperity 241
and green issues ix
growth vs environmental
degradation 65
hidden dependency on
environment 239–40
ecosystems, fragility of
239–40
electric vehicles 71–2, 90,
93–6
batteries 97–8, 99–100,
103
carbon deficit 100
carbon footprint of
electricity sources
100–1, 104
disadvantages of 96–7,
103–4
financial costs 101–3,
104
government policies
102–3
India 104–8
infrastructure 103–4
production footprint 98,
100
range anxiety 103
raw materials: cost 97
raw materials: recycled
97
raw materials: security of
supply 98
statistics 96
supply chains 96–7
United Kingdom 102–3,
105
vs conventional cars 98,
100–2
electricity 5. *see also* electric
vehicles
generation: fossil fuels
1–5, 19–20, 98, 100–1
generation: nuclear power
8, 10
generation: renewables
14–15, 20, 100–1
pricing 13, 101
taxes 24
Ellen MacArthur Foundation
35, 40
Emissions Trading System
(EU) 11, 169–70

energy companies
  green tariffs 22–3
  as integrated companies
    18, 74
  investments in 138–9
  name changes 19–20
  stranded assets 17–18
energy conservation xii
energy crisis, impact of
  xi–xii
energy density 15, 79
energy efficiency 11
Energy Performance
  Certificate 151–2
energy security 9, 10–11,
  65–6, 101
energy transitions x–xi, 3,
  23–5, 71
environment and economics
  64–5, 239–40
Environmental Audit
  Committee (2019) 49–50
Equinor 19
ESG (environment, society
  and governance)
  approach 137, 142, 150
ethanol 83
Ethereum blockchain system
  190–1
ethical exclusion 139–40
ethical investments 142,
  148–50
Ethiopia: textile industry 30
EU bloc
  and agriculture 169, 170
  carbon border adjustment
    mechanism 170
  cycling policies 110
  dependency on Russian
    gas 8
  Emissions Trading System
    11, 169–70
  fishing industry 218–20
  greenhouse gas emissions
    156
  job losses from weaning
    off coal 25
  net zero target viii–ix, 23
  and plastics 133
  recycling plastics 122
  single use plastic levies/
    bans 133
  steel industry 201, 204

tariffs for shipping
    companies 81
European Environment
  Agency 92
European Green Deal 23
Evergrande 205–6
exclusive economic zones
  (EEZs) 217
'exported' emissions 64
Extended Producer
  Responsibility
  legislation 122
externalities: textile industry
  36–7, 48
ExxonMobil 6, 17, 75, 79
  carbon capture and
    storage (CCS) 18, 78

F
fabrics
  cotton 28–9, 31, 32, 46
  ethically produced 32
  manufacturing process
    28–34
  natural 28–9
  recycled polyester 33
  recycling 32–3
  rPET (recycled plastics) in
    fabrics 32
  sustainable 33–4
  synthetic 28, 32, 33–4,
    35, 36
Facebook 191–2
Fairtrade coffee 176
Fairtrade cotton 32
Fancy, Tariq 142–4, 153–4
farming. see agriculture
fashion 34–7, 40. see also
  textile industry
Ferrell, Will 95
fertiliser 165–7, 169–70
financed emissions 136,
  146–7
financial services
  and climate change 136–8
  ethical investments
    148–50
  green mortgages 151
  greenwashing 144–8, 150
  investments 148–51
  net zero target 85, 143–5,
    146–7

pensions 148–50
shareholders 135, 139,
  141, 144, 147–8
Fink, Laurence Douglas
  137–8
fires vii
fishing industry 215–16. see
  also oceans
  bottom trawling 223
  bycatch 222–3
  and conservation 216–18
  EU bloc 218–20
  fish farms 223
  Morocco 220
  overfishing 216
  Peru 220–1
  regulation 217–22,
    226–7
  sustainability initiatives
    217–21
  United Kingdom 218–19
  water pollution 223
flexitarian diet 161
food industry 155–7
  agriculture 155–6,
    168–71
  carbon labelling 160–1
  China 172–3
  coffee 175–7
  fertiliser 165–7, 169–70
  food security 171–2,
    173–4
  greenhouse gas emissions
    156
  meat & dairy production
    157, 158–60
  meat substitutes 162–3
  sustainability initiatives
    175–7, 177–82
  waste management
    177–82
food security 171–2, 173–4
food waste 177–82
Ford 90, 95–6
Ford, Tom 131
forest fires: Europe &
  Canada vii
fossil fuels. see also coal
  alternatives to 76–9,
    83–4, 94–6
  global energy use 1–2
  transition away from at
    COP 28 (Dubai) x–xi

France
  agriculture 168
  air pollution 166–8
  gilet jaune protests 102
  reduction in beef
    consumption 162
fuel duty/taxes 102–3
Fukushima 9

G
gadgets. *see* phones
Gadkari, Nitin 104–5
gas
  liquid natural gas (LNG)
    76
  natural gas 4–5, 7–8
  price variation/spike
    2022: 8
  United Kingdom 7–8
GDP (Gross Domestic
  Product)
  disadvantages of 241–2
  and government policies
    244
  as a measure of prosperity
    241
  tracking energy use 3
General Motors 95
Ghana 210–11
glass bottles 127, 128
Glencore 56
global temperatures 1.5°C
  limit vii, viii, 62–3
global trade 69–72
global warming. *see* climate
  change
globalisation, consequences
  of vii–viii
Gobi Desert 58
Good on You (app) 47
government policies 92, 102–3
  agriculture 168–71
  car industry 92, 102–4,
    104–8, 112–13
  carbon taxes 24, 154, 201
  cycling 110
  European Green Deal
    19–21
  financial services 151,
    153–4
  fishing industry 222,
    226–7

food waste collections
    179
  and GDP 244
  'green' tax on electricity
    24
  investment in renewables
    11, 19–21
  and investment industry
    145–8
  and natural capital assets
    240–5
  plastic bag levies/bans
    131–3
  plastic waste 122–3
  provision for workers
    25
  public transport 109
  recycling plastic 121–2,
    123
  textile industry 48–50
graphite 98
Great Depression 73
Great Pacific Garbage Patch
    116
green energies. *see* renewable
  energy
green hydrogen 79, 84,
  86–7, 94
green tariffs 22–3
greenhouse gas emissions.
  see also fossil fuels
  building industry 197,
    199–200
  car industry 92, 100
  carbon sinks 224, 225–6
  China 61–2, 63–4, 203,
    204
  City of London 136
  electric vehicles 96–7
  energy production 2–3
  EU bloc 156
  fishing industry 223
  food industry 156
  food waste 177
  India 105
  Indonesia 234
  lithium ev batteries 98
  meat & dairy production
    157, 158–60
  net zero target viii–ix, 23,
    65, 146–7
  payment sector 183–4,
    186–7, 189–91

phone manufacture 54,
    55, 61
  shipping trade 71, 80, 81
  textile industry 27–8, 30
  United Kingdom 64
  United States 63–4
greenwashing
  financial services 144–8,
    150
  textile industry 44–6
grey hydrogen 78

H
H&M 40–1
hake 219–20
Hallet, Adrien 232
heat pumps 22
HeidelbergCement Norcem,
  Brevik 199
High Seas Treaty (2023)
    217–18
Hindmarch, Anya 133
homes: dependency on fossil
  fuels 1–2
HSBC 141, 147–8
hybrid cars 94–5
hydrogen fuel 16–17, 78–9,
  84, 86–7, 94, 201
hydropower 16

I
impact investing 149
income vs environmental
  degradation 64, 65
India
  building & construction
    industry 207
  car industry 104–8
  cotton production 28–30
  cycling policies 110
  fishing industry 221
  organic cotton 32
  phone manufacture 61
  public transport 109
  textile industry 28–30
Inditex: sustainability
  initiatives 41–3
individuals
  household energy use 2–3
  impact of green issues on
    ix–x

Indonesia 241–2
  deforestation 234
  fishing industry 221
  net zero target 234
  palm oil 233
Industrial Revolution 4–5
industrialisation 64
  China 61–2, 63–4, 73
  consequences of rapid
    increase vii–viii
  Kuznets curve 64
  United States 63–4, 73
industry: hidden dependency
  on environment
  239–40
Infinna 33
Institute of Positive Fashion
  48
International Chamber of
  Shipping: carbon levy
  81
International Council on
  Clean Transportation
  71
International Energy Agency
  14–15, 91
  projection for electric
    cars 96
  projection for global
    nuclear power 10
International Maritime
  Organization (IMO)
  and sulphur reduction
  80
investments
  and accountability 145–8
  ethical approach 142,
    148–50
  financed emissions 136–8
  government green policies
    145–8
  government policies
    145–8, 151
  green savings bonds 151
  greenwashing 144–8
  impact investing 149
  net zero financed
    emissions target 139
  pension funds 148–50
  responsible investing
    139–41
IT: information on
  consumers 36

J
Japan 7
  building & construction
    industry 205
  nuclear plants 9
  recycling plastics 122
Jedlik, Ányos 90
John Lewis 39

K
Kay, Arthur 180
Kerry, John 81
Kirby, Scott 84
Kuznets curve 64–5, 208,
  211, 234
Kuznets, Simon 241

L
landfill 67, 128
  clothing waste 35–6,
    38, 49
  food waste 179
  methane emissions 118,
    124, 129, 179
  plastic waste 118, 129,
    131–2
laptops 54
Lever, Lord William 231
Libra Association 191–2
linear economy: textile
  industry 39–40
liquid natural gas (LNG) 76
lithium
  alternatives to 107
  ev batteries 97–8, 99–100
  from geothermal water
    99
  mining for 55–6
  phone batteries 55–6
  recycling lithium batteries
    99–100
living standards,
  improvements in 5
Lloyds of London 140
Loliware 131
London
  City of London carbon
    footprint 136
  transport initiatives 102,
    110, 111
L'Oréal 130

Lyft 111–12
Lyocell 33–4

M
Macron, President 168
Maersk
  net zero target 81
  use of methanol fuel 76–7
make-do-and-mend mindset
  xii, 179
Make My Money Matter
  149
Malaysia
  deforestation 234
  palm oil 232–3
  plastic waste 118
manganese: ev batteries 98
mangroves: blue carbon
  225–6
market forces 7, 151–3, 162
McDonald's 130
meat production
  Brazil 157–8
  environmental impact
    158–60
  greenhouse gas emissions
    157, 158–60
  meat substitutes 162–3
methane emissions 76
  capture at landfill sites
    124
  capture from coffee
    grounds 179–80
  capture from landfill 124,
    179
  China 63, 173
  from cows 158–60
methanol 76–7
microparticles 167
microplastics 134
  plastic waste 35, 117–18,
    134
  synthetic fabrics 35
  water pollution 35, 117,
    134
Middle East 5–6
milk alternatives 164
mobile phones. see phones
Monbiot, George 245
money. see also payment
  sector
  ATMs 184

banknotes 184–5, 230
cash vs card payments
183–7
coins 184
Morocco
cobalt mining 99
fishing industry 220
mortgages 151–2
Mountain Pass, California 60
multinationals: sustainability
initiatives 85
Musk, Elon 190–1

N

naphtha 116
National Grid 12, 23, 104
natural capital assets 242–6
natural fabrics 28–9, 33
natural gas 4–5, 7–8
liquid natural gas (LNG)
76
natural world. *see*
environment
Neom, Saudi Arabia 86
Nestlé 119, 121, 237
Net Zero Banking Alliance
139
net zero target 65–6, 139,
146–7
China 65
EU bloc viii–ix, 23
financial services 85,
143–5, 146–7
Indonesia 234
multinationals 85
United States 81
New Zealand: Living
Standards Framework
244
news, negative bias xi
NFTs (non-fungible tokens)
191
Nissan Leaf 103
nitrous oxides 92, 93, 159,
166–7
North Atlantic fishing
218–19
North Sea cod 218
North Sea Oil 20–1
Norway
electric powered public
transport 108

fishing industry 218, 219
gas exports 8
invests in energy
companies 19
nuclear disasters 9
nuclear energy 8–10
nuclear waste 9

O

Oatly 160, 164
Ocean Cleanup 117–18
oceans. *see also* fishing
industry
acidification 224
benefits of 215
as carbon sinks 224,
225–6
and climate change 224–5
conservation of 217,
225–7
exclusive economic zones
(EEZs) 217
rising sea levels 224–5
as shared resources
216–17
sustainability initiatives
225–6
temperature increases 224
oil
alternatives to 76–9
and car industry 89
energy density 15, 72
oil industry 4–5
demands rising 74
North Sea oil 20–1
price variation/spike 1970s
10–11
response to climate change
6
and transport 70, 71
United States 74
oil majors. *see* energy
companies
oil prices
1970s crisis 10–11
2022 spike 73, 75
and traders' speculations
73–4
Om Organic Cotton 32
online payments 187
online shopping 35–6
OPEC 10–11

Open Banking 187
Ørsted: transition to
renewable energy 20
Ortega, Amancio 41
Oslo: electric powered public
transport 108
Oxfam 38

P

palm oil 246
accountability 236–8
consumer awareness
234–5, 236
names for 230
origins 231
supply and demand
economics 238–9
sustainability initiatives
235–8
versatility 229–31
Paris Agreement (2015)
viii–ix, 62–3
consequences for stranded
assets 17–18
and oil consumption 70
Paris: air pollution 166–8
Patagonia 36–7
payment sector. *see also*
money
bitcoin 184, 188–94
cryptocurrencies 184,
188–94
global 186
greenhouse gas emissions
183–4, 186–7, 189–91
online payments 187
Pemberton, John S. 119
pension funds 148–50
PepsiCo 119, 121
Perez, Bea 126–7, 128
Peru: fishing industry
220–1
pesticides
coffee production 176
food industry 156, 165
textile industry 28, 32
PET (polyethylene
terephthalate) 116
fizzy drinks bottles
119–21
recycling problems
120–2

phones
  batteries 55–6
  benefits of 53–4, 66–7
  carbon footprint 55
  child labour 56
  cobalt use 56–7
  dependence on China for
    resources 66
  greenhouse gas emissions
    54
  lithium batteries 55–6
  manufacture 61–6
  ownership statistics 54
  production 55
  rare earth metals 57–61
  resources used 54–61
  supply chains 56
  sustainability initiatives
    67–8
  waste 54
PLA (polylactic acid)
  129–30
PlantBottle 129
plastic waste
  and Covid-19 pandemic
    xi
  exporting 122–4
  fizzy drinks bottles
    119–20
  government policies
    131–3
  laminates 123
  microplastics 35, 117–18,
    134
  recycling 121–2, 124–5
  rPET (recycled plastics)
    32, 121, 124–5
  statistics 116–17
  water pollution 35,
    116–18, 134
plastics 116
  alternatives to 126–31
  plant based 129
plastics industry 125–6
Poland: job losses 25
Polasky, Stephen 243
pollution
  microplastics 35, 117,
    134
  shipping trade 71
  water pollution 29–30,
    35, 55–6, 116–18, 134,
    223

polyester, recycled 33
polymerisation 116
polysilicon 13
Poshmark 38–9
'price elasticity' 37
prices
  consumer sensitivity to 37
  surges in due to
    commodities supercycles
    72–3
public awareness of global
  warming 5
public transport 108–9,
  112

Q
Qatar: exporter of liquid
  gas 8

R
rainforest 158
  conservation vs income
    239
  loss of 233–4
  and sustainable palm oil
    235–8
Rana Plaza factory 30, 50
range anxiety 103
rare earth metals
  China 57–9, 61
  phones 57–61
  United States v China
    trade war 59–60
raw materials, increased
  demand for 72–3
recycling
  batteries 99–100
  clothing 38–9
  food waste 181–2
  plastic waste 120–2,
    124–5
refillable containers 130
remote working xi
'renewable certificates' 23
renewable energy x, xii, 7.
    see also individual types
  China 66
  costs fall in 21st century
    14–15
  energy companies invest
    in 18, 74

government policies 11,
    19–21
  increased interest in after
    1970s 11
  limitations of 15, 21
  textile industry 42–3
  United Kingdom 12, 14
  United States 14–15
Rent the Runway 38–9
responsible investing
  139–41
retail
  excess stock burned 40,
    49
  focus on profit 37
  marketing tactics 36,
    44–5
  obligation to shareholders
    37
  overproduction 39–40
  price increase to reflect
    'externalities' 36
  sustainability challenges
    39–43
rice 173–4
Rockefeller, John D. 75
Rose, Alison 142
Roundtable on Sustainable
  Palm Oil (RSPO)
    235–8
Royal Bank of Scotland
    141–2
Royal Botanic Garden Kew
    175–6
rPET (recycled plastics) 32,
    121, 124–5
Russia
  exporter of gas 8
  fishing industry 221
  invasion of Ukraine 2022:
    9, 73, 171, 172, 231
Rust Belt (USA) 125, 203

S
salt marshes: blue carbon
    225–6
Satoshi Nakamoto 188
Saudi Arabia
  dependence on oil industry
    85–6
  green hydrogen plant
    86–7

oil price crisis 1970s
10–11
and shipping fuel 80
sea-grass: blue carbon
225–6
SEA Technology 131
seas. *see* oceans
seaweed-based straws 130–1
Senegal 211
the Seven Sisters 6
shale extraction: United
States 74
shareholders
financial services 135,
139, 141, 144, 147–8
textile industry 37
sharing economy 111
Sharma, Alok 63
Shell 6, 18, 19, 180
Shetland Islands: Viking
wind farm 12
shipping trade 69–70
alternative fuels 76–9
greenhouse gas emissions
71, 80, 81
hidden costs of 70–2
oil consumption 70, 71
sulphur reduction 80
sustainability initiatives
76–9
zero carbon fuel pledges
85
shopping, online
clothing rental & resale
sites 38–9
consumer data used by
retailers 36
disadvantages of 35–6, 39
waste sent to landfill
35–6, 39
Sierra Leone 175–6
smartphones. *see* phones
Sococim 211
solar energy 13, 14, 15, 21
SolarCoin 193
South Korea 181–2
Sri Lanka: textile industry
32
Standard Oil 75
state investment. *see*
government policies
Statoil 19
steel 199–201, 211–13

alternatives to 211–13
China 202–4
EU bloc 201, 204
importance of 196
United States 203
stranded assets 17–18,
138–9
straws 130–1
sugar prices vii
sulphur reduction: shipping
trade 80
Sumatra: palm oil 232
Sunak, Rishi 146
sunflower oil 231
Sunnylands Statement (2023)
63, 65
supply chains
complexity of 45–6, 47
electric vehicles 96–7
move closer to place of
production xi
phone industry 56
sustainability challenges
phones 54–61, 67
textile industry 36–43
sustainability initiatives
aviation industry 82–4
fishing industry 217–21
multinationals 85
phones 67–8
shipping trade 76–9
textile industry 41–3, 47
SUVs 91
Sweden: rare earth metals
60–1
synthetic fabrics 28, 32,
35, 36

T

tablets (technology) 54
Tata Motors 107
taxes
and car industry 102–3
carbon taxes 24, 154, 201
Plastic Packaging Tax
(2022) 50
taxis 111–12
Tesco 160
Tesla 99, 190
Textil Baskstil 47
textile industry 34–6, 47
accountability 44–7

bio-based synthetic
polymers 33–4
circular economy 38–40,
51
cotton 28–9, 31, 32
in developing countries
29–30, 46–7
discount sales 40
dyeing 29
effects of cheap fast
fashion 34–6
ethically produced
synthetics 32
externalities 36–7, 48
global nature of 29–32,
37–8, 46–7
greenhouse gas emissions
27–8
greenwashing 44–6
lack of accountability
44–7
linear economy 39–40
luxury brands 37, 40
manufacturing process
28–34
overproduction 39–40, 43
pressure from consumers
43–5
price increases to reflect
'externalities' 36–7, 48
production 28–34, 46–7
recycling fabrics 32–3
renewable energy sources
42–3
role of government to
ensure sustainability
48–50
rPET (recycled plastics) in
fabrics 32
supply chains 45–6, 47
sustainability challenges
36–43
sustainability initiatives
41–3, 47
transport 31
waste 31
water use 28–30
workers spread globally
29–32, 37–8, 46–7
Tibet: lithium production
55–6
Total 18
toxic waste 9, 57–61

transition to renewable energy 23–5
transport. *see also* car industry
aviation 81–4
cargo ships 70–2
green hydrogen 86–7
hydrogen fuel 16–17, 78–9, 84, 86–7
public transport 108–9
shipping cargo 69–72
textile industry 31
zero carbon fuel pledges 85
Trump, President 203
Turkey: imported waste 122–3

U
Uber 111–12
Ukraine: invasion by Russia 2022 9, 73, 171, 172, 231
United Airlines 83, 84
United Kingdom
car industry 102–3, 105
cash vs card payments 183–6
Clean Air Act (1956) 7
electric vehicles 102–3, 105
'exported' emissions 64
exported waste 123
financial services 151–2, 153–4
fishing industry 218
food waste 178–9
green tariffs 22–3
greenhouse gas emissions 64
heat pump subsidies 22
move towards renewable energy 7
nuclear energy 8–9
public transport 108, 109
recycling plastics 122
reduction in meat consumption 161
single use plastic levies/bans 132–3
solar energy 21

transition to gas post World War 2 7–8
ULEZ (Ultra Low Emissions Zone) scheme 102
wind energy 11, 12, 14
United Nations Convention on the Law of the Sea (UNCLOS) 217
United States
cash vs card payments 186
effects of cheap fast fashion 35–6
Environmental Protection Agency 92–3
exported waste 124
fishing industry 221
food waste 178
greenhouse gas emissions 63–4
Inflation Reduction Act (2022) x, xi, 15, 78–9, 96, 125–6
nuclear plants 8–9
plastic collection problems 121–2
plastic production 125–6
plastic waste 118–19
rare earth metal supplies 59–60
renewable energy production increases 14
shale extraction 74
shipping trade 80, 81
single use plastic levies/bans 132
stranded assets 17–18
trade war with China 59–60, 203
wind energy 11, 14
wind turbine subsidies 22
uranium 8
urbanisation 195–6, 202

V
Vietnam
fishing industry 221
phone manufacture 61
rice production 173–4

Viking wind farm 12
Vinted x, 38–9
Volkswagen: toxic diesel cars 93

W
Wastesaver 38
water pollution 29–30, 35
fishing industry 223
lithium 55–6
microplastics 35, 117, 134
plastic waste 116–18
textile industry 29–30, 35
water use
food production 156, 173
phone industry 55
textile industry 28–9
wind energy
Denmark 20
limitations 15
personal wind turbines 22
problems 12–13
United Kingdom 11, 12, 14
United States 11, 14
wind farms 12–13
wind turbines 13, 22
Woods, Darren 79
workers
child labour 56
phone industry 56
provision for in transitions 25
textile industry 30
World Economic Forum 2020 126–7, 239–40
World Trade Organization 222
Wyeth, Nathaniel 119

X
Xi, Jinping 62
Xiaoping, Deng 57

Z
Zara 41–3, 46–7
Zipcar 111

Viking wind farm 12
Vimed x, 58-9
Volkswagen toxic diesel
    cars 93

W
Watersaver 38
water pollution 29-30, 3
    fishing industry 221
    lithium 55-6
    microplastics 35, 117
    134
    plastic waste 116-18
    textile industry 29-30,
    35
water use
    food production 136-
    phone industry 55
    textile industry 28-9
wind energy
    Denmark 20
    installations 13
    personal wind turbines
    22
    problems 12-13
    United Kingdom 11
    12, 13
    United States 11, 13
    wind farms 12-13
    wind turbines 12, 22
workers
    child labour 56
    phone industry 56
    provision for in transition
    35
    textile industry 30,
World Economic Forum
    2020 126-7, 134-42
World Trade Organization
    221
Wroth, Nathaniel 114

X
Xi Jinping 62
Xiaoping, Deng

Z
Zara 41-3, 46-7
Zipar 111